THE COMMON CORE STATE STANDARDS IN LITERACY SERIES

A series designed to help educators successfully
implement CCSS literacy standards in K–12 classrooms

SUSAN B. NEUMAN AND D. RAY REUTZEL, EDITORS

SERIES BOARD: Diane August, Linda Gambrell, Steve Graham, Laura Justice,
Margaret McKeown, and Timothy Shanahan

Helping English Learners to Write

Carol Booth Olson
Robin C. Scarcella
Tina Matuchniak

Foreword by Steve Graham

Meeting Common Core Standards, Grades 6–12

TEACHERS COLLEGE PRESS
TEACHERS COLLEGE | COLUMBIA UNIVERSITY
NEW YORK AND LONDON

NATIONAL WRITING PROJECT
2105 Bancroft Way, #1042
Berkeley, CA 94720

tesol
international
association
1925 Ballenger Avenue
Alexandria, VA 22314 USA

Published simultaneously by Teachers College Press, 1234 Amsterdam Avenue, New York, NY 10027 and TESOL International Association, 1925 Ballenger Avenue, Alexandria, VA 22314 USA and National Writing Project, 2105 Bancroft Way, Berkeley, CA 94720-1042.

The National Writing Project (NWP) is a nationwide network of educators working together to improve the teaching of writing in the nation's schools and in other settings. NWP provides high-quality professional development programs to teachers in a variety of disciplines and at all levels, from early childhood through university. Through its network of nearly 200 university-based sites, NWP develops the leadership, programs and research needed for teachers to help students become successful writers and learners.

Hetty Jun's letter: Olson, Carol Booth, *Reading/Writing Connection, The: Strategies for Teaching and Learning in the Secondary Classroom*, 3rd, © 2011. Printed and electronically reproduced by permission of Pearson Education, Inc., Upper Saddle River, New Jersey.

Figure 4.1: Tompkins, Gail E. Literacy For the 21st Century: A Balanced Approach, 6th Ed., © 2014. Printed and electronically reproduced by permission of Pearson Education, Inc., Upper Saddle River, New Jersey.

Figure 5.5: Illustrations by Kathleen Borowick. Reprinted by Permission of David R. Godine, Publisher, Inc. Copyright © 1982 Lawrence Treat, Illustrations by Kathleen Borowick.

Library of Congress Cataloging-in-Publication Data is available at loc.gov

ISBN 978-0-8077-5633-1 (paper)
ISBN 978-0-8077-7367-3 (ebook)

Printed on acid-free paper
Manufactured in the United States of America

22 21 20 19 18 17 16 15   8 7 6 5 4 3 2 1

Contents

Foreword

There is no shortage of advice on how to improve other people's writing. Professional writers are particularly fond of giving tips, offering counsel that runs the gamut from helpful ("A short story must have a single mood and every sentence builds towards it." Edgar Allan Poe) to fanciful ("When you catch an adjective, kill it." Mark Twain) to ridiculous ("Hitch your unconscious mind to your writing arm." Dorothea Brande). Perhaps my favorite tip from a professional writer is: ". . . don't listen to any advice given by writers." I found this recommendation singularly amusing, as it was given by picture book writer, Jon Scieszka.

Nowhere is good advice needed more than with learning how to write. This is one of the hardest things that students must learn to master. Writing involves solving a problem. Sometimes the focus of the problem is very clear, such as writing an email to convince a friend that you should see a specific movie. At other times, the problem may be less clear, such as writing an engaging story to share with your nephew on his 6th birthday.

If we analyze either of these writing tasks closely, we find that writing is anything but simple. Take for instance the more straightforward problem of convincing your friend you should see a particular movie. You may initially know some, and maybe even all of the basic points you want to make in your email, but you still have to decide how to express, organize, and elevate these ideas so that you persuade your friend, which will require the use of a variety of cognitive, motor, and affective skills. You have to decide what to say and how to say it; make multiple judgments about how to turn your intentions into sentences; select just the right words to convey the intended meaning; ensure that words are correctly spelled and sentences are grammatically correct; and evaluate and possibly revise your emerging message so it is forceful and clear.

While the example above captures some of the complexities involved in writing and learning to write, it does not address the writing challenges faced by adolescents in schools in the United States who are just learning to speak English or are still involved in mastering its complexities. English learners are a diverse group, coming from many different cultures, with varying degrees of experience in learning how to write, and speaking languages that differ widely in their similarities to English. This diversity and these differences require that we provide the very best writing instruction we can for these students.

So how do we make this a reality? If I drew up my dream scenario for achieving this goal, it would involve two basic ingredients. First, writing instruction for these students would include the application of instructional procedures with a proven track record of success. In other words, writing practices that have been scientifically tested and validated as improving the writing of English learners. Second, I would draw on the expertise of master teachers, with considerable experience teaching writing to these students, to flesh out a writing program that blends evidence-based practices with the considerable lore on how to teach writing gathered over the years.

So imagine how pleased I was when asked to write the foreword to this book. My dream became a reality. Authors Carol Booth Olson, Robin C. Scarcella, and Tina Matuchniak, are at the very forefront of scientifically testing and validating instructional practices for improving the writing and reading of adolescents who are English learners. Why is their research so good? It is informed by years of experience in the classroom and working with hundreds of teachers across California. What a powerful combination.

My advice: Ingest, consider, and employ the strategies described here. Your students will become better writers if you do.

—Steve Graham,
Warner Professor of Educational Leadership & Innovation,
Arizona State University

Preface

Designed for classroom teachers, graduate students, literacy specialists, researchers, and interested members of the general public, this book offers a rich array of research-based practices to improve the academic writing of English learners (ELs).

Currently, ELs are the fastest growing group of school-age children in the United States and constitute approximately 10% of the total K–12 population (U.S. Department of Education, Institute of Education Sciences, National Center for Education Statistics, 2012a). At the same time that EL enrollments have increased in U.S. public schools, researchers and policymakers have highlighted large literacy gaps based on students' English language proficiency. Results from the National Assessment of Educational Progress (NAEP) indicate that the poor reading and writing performance of ELs in the middle grades persists through high school. The 2011 administration of the NAEP revealed a significant gap between the computer-based English writing of 8th-grade ELs and their non-EL peers, with less than 1% of ELs at both 8th grade and 12th grade scoring at the proficient level (U.S. Department of Education, Institute of Education Sciences, National Center for Education Statistics, 2012b). Such status reports, coupled with the increasing numbers of ELs, suggest that serious attention must be paid to determine how best to enhance the academic literacy of ELs in secondary school.

Adolescent ELs must, at the same time, grapple with the demands of learning an additional language, negotiate the nuances of academic discourse, and master core subject matter. While all learners may face many constraints when learning to write, the difficulties ELs face are magnified because they have to compose in a second language. Teachers need effective instructional practices to help them. These practices can enable ELs to read, negotiate, and understand complex texts independently and produce thoughtful and nuanced writing that is well-reasoned and supported with evidence. These are the skills and abilities the Common Core State Standards (CCSS) for English Language Arts and Literacy in History/Social Studies, Science, and Technical Subjects call for all students, including ELs, to master in order to become college and

---

career ready (National Governors Association Center for Best Practices & Council of Chief State School Officers, 2010).

Adopted by 46 states, the CCSS present a vision of what it means to be literate in the 21st century and call for all students, including ELs, to develop critical reading skills necessary for a deep understanding of complex texts, and critical writing skills needed to write about those texts. In addition to delineating specific standards for each grade level, the CCSS include College and Career Readiness Anchor Standards for Reading and Writing. As is evident from the anchor standards, the CCSS set a high bar for *all* students and prioritize the ability to analyze and interpret challenging texts and to write about those texts using academic discourse in extended pieces of writing. For EL students, many of whom have been in classrooms focused on literal comprehension and short-answer responses, meeting these rigorous new standards can be daunting. In fact, researchers have noted a "growing inequality" in classrooms where students designated as "honors students" are exposed to rigorous academic work designed to promote higher literacy, whereas low achievers, children of the poor, and ELs often receive instruction that emphasizes the "transmission of information, providing very little room for the exploration of ideas, which is necessary for the development of deeper understanding" (Applebee, Langer, Nystrand, & Gamoran, 2003, p. 689). Given the many demands that academic writing places on them and the lack of practice many ELs have as academic writers, ELs face significant challenges as they strive to become college and career ready.

Although the CCSS acknowledge that ELs may require additional time and instructional support as they acquire English language proficiency and content knowledge, the standards look to teachers to provide "whatever tools and knowledge their professional judgment and experience identify as most helpful for meeting the goals set out in the standards" (National Governors Association, p. 4). This makes it imperative for teachers to identify effective ways of teaching ELs.

This book addresses the tools and knowledge teachers need in order to enhance the academic writing of ELs. It provides specific teaching strategies, activities, and extended lessons to develop ELs' narrative, informational, and argumentative writing as well as explores the challenges each of these genres poses for ELs and suggests ways to scaffold instruction to help ELs become confident and competent academic writers. Showcasing the work of exemplary teachers who have devoted time and expertise to creating rich learning environments for ELs, it also includes artifacts and written work produced by students with varying levels of language proficiency as models of what students can accomplish.

Readers can use this book to:

- Become better informed about best practices for teaching writing to ELs
- Plan and set goals for instruction
- Supplement existing English language arts or English language development curricula with research-based strategies, activities, and lessons
- Develop a community of learners
- Create safe classroom spaces in which students are encouraged to participate, even with less-than-perfect English
- Design and implement culturally responsive instruction, building on students' strengths
- Help ELs meet the Common Core State Standards

Although most of the instructional practices described in this book are intended for ELs in English language arts classrooms who have expanding-to-advanced levels of English proficiency, teachers also will find practices that have been designed for ELs with an emerging level of English proficiency. Also included are practices for teaching recent arrivals to the United States as well as students who have lived in the United States for many years.

Helping English Learners to Write—Meeting Common Core Standards, Grades 6–12 is divided into five chapters. Each chapter begins with a brief overview and ends with a short summary of the key points.

Chapter 1, "English Learners: Who Are They, and What Do They Need to Meet the Common Core Standards for Writing?" provides an overview of English learners—their diversity, the challenges they face, and what they need to know and be able to do in order to succeed in secondary school. The chapter discusses the multiple constraints faced by ELs, including but not limited to cognitive, linguistic, communicative, contextual, textual, affective, and cultural constraints. Each of these constraints makes additional and competing demands on learners' working memory, which can confound the learning process. This is especially true in relation to the Common Core Standards for English Language Arts (CCSS/ELA), which place a premium on analyzing and interpreting challenging texts and using academic discourse in extended pieces of writing. This chapter sets the stage for what teachers can do to help ELs meet the CCSS.

Chapter 2, "Best Practices for Teaching Writing to English Learners," summarizes the current research on writing instruction for English learners and suggests some commonly accepted best practices for teaching writing to ELs: creating culturally relevant writing instruction in a community of learners; strategy instruction; modeling with mentor texts; explicit instruction in academic language; scaffolding instruction; and using formative assessment for developing future instruction. Each of these best practices is illustrated with accompanying strategies, activities, and lessons that both scholars and practitioners alike will find useful. The chapter concludes by emphasizing the importance of providing ELs with ample opportunities to practice what they have learned.

Chapter 3, "Narrative Writing and CCSS," is dedicated to narrative writing and begins with an explanation of the importance of this genre not only in helping ELs to convey their experiences, but also in serving as a gateway into other genres such as informational and argumentative writing. The chapter outlines the language demands of narrative writing and the challenges that ELs may face in mastering this genre. It describes the elements of narrative writing—sequencing, showing, not telling, vocabulary of the senses, to name just a few—and provides multiple lessons and activities to illustrate how each element might be taught. The chapter provides several prompts for writing narratives and concludes with a lesson on how to blend narrative writing with other genres of writing.

Chapter 4, "Informative/Explanatory Texts and CCSS," begins with a summary of the language demands of this genre and the challenges that ELs might face when engaging it. The chapter discusses how to teach the various text structures involved in reading and writing informational texts, such as description, sequence, comparison/contrast, cause/effect, and problem/solution, and provides helpful lessons and activities to accompany each one. The chapter further provides high-interest activities that reinforce essential skills such as summary writing, as well as more current and complex skills such as developing podcasts, becoming investigative journalists, and using project-based learning.

Chapter 5, "Argumentative Writing and CCSS," begins with a discussion of the importance of argumentative writing in the context of the CCSS. It explains the various types of argumentative writing that secondary school students typically engage in and describes the elements of the genre. The chapter discusses macroconcerns of the genre, such as using evidence and commentary to develop arguments, as well as acknowledging and refuting counterarguments. It also discusses microconcerns, such as how to properly integrate quotations and use action verbs, appositives, participles, and other grammatical devices to create vivid language. The chapter includes a section on how to transform informal language into academic English and concludes with a scaffolded lesson on how to teach the argumentative essay.

This book aims to synthesize the current research on ELs and writing in addition to summarizing the best practices for classroom instruction. We hope that in these pages readers will find information that will lead to new research and enhance classroom instruction to better serve English learners in secondary schools.

CHAPTER 1

English Learners
Who Are They, and What Do They Need to Meet the Common Core Standards for Writing?

Marisela Gonzalez[1] is a 12-year-old student attending 6th grade in a large urban middle school, where 98% of the students are Chicano/Latino and 88% are designated as English learners. An immigrant from Mexico, Marisela arrived in the United States at the age of 6. She first was enrolled in English Language Development for bilingual learners and later in elementary school was transitioned into mainstream English language arts. Marisela speaks Spanish at home, and she is quite fluent in conversational English due to her many years of exposure to English in school. However, she is still struggling to acquire academic English, and her writing reflects her struggle. At the beginning of the school year, to assess the writing ability of Marisela and her classmates, her teacher, Ms. Maria Gómez-Greenberg, read an article to the students about an earthquake in Haiti entitled "Sometimes, the Earth Is Cruel," by award-winning journalist Leonard Pitts (2010). She asked the students to follow along silently as she read aloud. After clarifying the meaning of difficult vocabulary words and discussing the article, she gave them 50 minutes to write an analytical essay about the author's theme in the text and also to discuss how he used both literal and figurative language to convey his meaning. Marisela wrote the following:

> In this story there was alot of people that sufferd. People died and suf-
> ferd from all the earthquakes. Also, littel boys and girls parents died.
> People had to reboit their houses when they Gought destroyed. Alot
> of people sufferd because every year there was an earthquake. It only
> happened to haiti that why people were tired of it. After the arthquack
> happened people were very bore. It was very bad alot people died over
> 100,000 people died this last earthquack. Sometimes when it raind it

1. We have used a pseudonym for this student, who was a participant in a research study.

will not stop for days. Sometimes the earth was cruel, but they had no choice but to exept it. That is how much the sufferd. When people died the dig there selfes they weep and mourn we recover and memoriaize the dead. People also got very sick and neded medisen. People use to pray that begins, "There, but for the grace of good . . . ." People did everything they can. People use to write relief checks, donate blood, volunteer material and time and to fear. That what people did to help people that were very sick. Thats why we should be happy to be safe. This story is a good example. so people can see what will happen if that was us. Also, people can help and doneate stuff like close, shoes, meony, old stuff, to us. I think we should do that to help our people that are very sick. alot of of people died of bing hongry because the earth quake distroyed there homes and there food. (Fitzgerald, Olson, Garcia, & Scarcella, 2014, p. 216).

The purpose of this book is to help teachers like Ms. Gómez-Greenberg to prepare students like Marisela to enhance her academic literacy so that she can read, negotiate, and understand complex texts independently and produce thoughtful and nuanced writing that is well-reasoned and supported with evidence. These are the skills and abilities the Common Core State Standards (CCSS) for English Language Arts and Literacy in History/Social Studies, Science, and Technical Subjects call for all students, including English learners, to master in order to become college and career ready (National Governors Association, 2010).

WHO ARE ENGLISH LEARNERS?

The nation lacks a uniform definition and classification of English learners. Hence, ELs are called many names, including English language learners, limited English proficient students, language or linguistic minority students, and second language learners. Forty years ago, many viewed ELs as a relatively homogeneous group with similar instructional needs. This stereotype has endured despite large demographic changes. However, ELs today are a diverse group with unique experiences and backgrounds (Harklau, Losey, & Siegal, 1999; Matsuda, Ortmeier-Hooper, & You, 2006).

One group of secondary ELs, for example, consists of recent immigrants to the United States, often called newcomers, who have lived in the United States a short time. Newcomers vary in terms of their knowledge of English. Those with emerging English proficiency benefit from considerable background information as well as educational and linguistic resources in order to access texts and write them effectively, even when they have received formal education in their home countries. They require accelerated, intensive English instruction and, because of federal law (*Lau v. Nichols*, 1973), are not mainstreamed into regular English language arts classes. Newcomers with developing levels of English proficiency who find themselves in mainstreamed English language arts classrooms often have pressing, short-term needs for support to help them acclimatize to the instructional contexts in which they find themselves in the United States. For instance, they gain greatly from guidance that helps them understand the self-reliance and individualism emphasized in American schools. Some may expect their teachers to be responsible for regularly reminding them of the due dates of homework assignments, giving them written summaries of key points, and preventing their plagiarizing. This is because the roles of teachers and student expectations of teachers vary from one culture to the next, and newcomers often view American teachers from their previous experiences.

Currently, ELs are the fastest growing segment of school-age children in the United States and constitute approximately 10% of the total K–12 population (U.S. Department of Education, Institute of Education Sciences, National Center for Education Statistics, 2012a). Although ELs in the United States speak more than 350 languages, 73% speak Spanish as their first language (Batalova & McHugh 2010), 40% have origins in Mexico (Hernandez, Denton, & Macartney, 2008), and 60% of ELs in grades 6 through 12 come from low-income families (Batalova, Fix, & Murray, 2007; Capps et al., 2005). At the same time that EL enrollments have increased in U.S. public schools, researchers and policymakers have highlighted large literacy gaps based on students' English language proficiency. Results from the NAEP indicate that the poor reading and writing performance of ELs in the middle grades persists through high school. The 2011 administration of the NAEP revealed a significant gap between the computer-based English writing of 8th-grade ELs and their non-EL peers, with less than 1% of ELs at both 8th grade and 12th grade scoring at the proficient level (U.S. Department of Education, Institute of Education Sciences, National Center for Education Statistics, 2012b). Such status reports, coupled with the increasing numbers of students for whom English is a second language, suggest that serious attention must be paid to determine how best to enhance the academic literacy of ELs in secondary school.

The largest numbers of ELs in our schools today are referred to as long-term English learners or LTELs (Menken & Kleyn, 2009). According to Olsen (2010), these are students who have been educated in the United States since age 6, are doing poorly in school, and have major gaps in knowledge because their schooling was disrupted. In Olsen's study of 175,734 ELs, the majority (59%) were LTELs who were failing to acquire academic language and struggling to do well in high school. They may come from homes where the primary language is not English, but they themselves may speak English only or they may switch between multiple languages *and* still have features in their writing attesting to their multilingual status (Valdés, 2001). These students are limited in their knowledge of academic registers in any language and have restricted knowledge of the world. They often are mainstreamed into regular English language arts classrooms.

A similar group of ELs consists of Generation 1.5 immigrants (Roberge, Siegal, & Harklau, 2009; Schleppegrell, 2009). Generation 1.5 immigrants refer specifically to college-age immigrants who come to the United States at a very young age but, although they receive much of their education in the United States, have not yet mastered the linguistic features and patterns that are used in academic settings at the college level. Some may come from specific racial or ethnic enclaves, while others may not. Like LTELs, they may have subtle but important gaps in their knowledge and experience and may exhibit "typical" ESL features, such as the absence of inflectional endings and the modal auxiliary verbs *could, should,* and *might.*

It is important to point out that many ELs arrive in school extremely proficient in English and in writing. They often enter classrooms with knowledge of the academic registers of a variety of languages and a wide range of background knowledge on scholarly topics. Hence, it is important for teachers to resist taking a deficit view of ELs, regardless of their backgrounds.

Since ELs are such a diverse group, K–12 schools and teachers across the nation face a much more wide-ranging student population than they did 30 years ago. We focus on the ELs who have developing-to-advanced levels of English proficiency and are diverse in terms of their educational, linguistic, and cultural backgrounds, and who have mainstreamed into regular English language arts classrooms.

WHAT ARE ENGLISH LEARNERS EXPECTED TO KNOW
AND BE ABLE TO DO IN SECONDARY SCHOOL?

Many content teachers of ELs avoid teaching their students to read strategically and to engage in text-based academic writing, such as composing analytical essays, because they think the skills required are too sophisticated for the population they serve. Yet, more than half of all states have established high-stakes graduation exams that assess high-level reading and writing abilities (Horwitz et al., 2009). A study of prototype test items for high school exit exams across the nation (Wong Fillmore & Snow, 2003) reveals the degree of academic literacy expected of all secondary students, including ELs, whose performance is assessed on a range of complex tasks, including summarizing texts, using linguistic cues to interpret and infer the writer's intentions and messages, assessing the writer's use of language for rhetorical and aesthetic purposes, evaluating evidence and arguments presented in texts, and composing and writing extended, reasoned texts that are supported with evidence.

Adopted by 46 states, the Common Core State Standards present a vision of what it means to be literate in the 21st century and call for all students, including ELs, to develop critical reading skills necessary for a deep understanding of complex texts and critical writing skills needed to write about those texts. In addition to specifying standards for each grade level, the CCSS include College and Career Readiness (CCR) Anchor Standards for Reading and Writing in grades K–5 and grades 6–12 that define the skills and understandings all students must demonstrate. Figure 1.1 presents the CCR for Reading. Figure 1.2 shows the CCR for Writing.

As is evident from these anchor standards, the CCSS set a high bar for all students and place a premium on the ability to analyze and interpret challenging texts and to write about those texts using academic discourse in extended pieces of writing. For EL students, many of whom have been in classrooms focused on literal comprehension and short-answer responses, meeting these rigorous new standards can be daunting. In fact, researchers have noted a "growing inequality" in classrooms where students designated as "honors students" are exposed to rigorous academic work designed to promote higher literacy, whereas low achievers, children of the poor, and second language learners often receive instruction that places a premium on the "transmission of information, providing very little room for the exploration of ideas, which is necessary for the development of deeper understanding" (Applebee et al., 2003, p.

Figure 1.1. College and Career Readiness Anchor Standards for Reading

Key Ideas and Details

1. Read closely to determine what the text says explicitly and to make logical inferences from it; cite specific textual evidence when writing or speaking to support conclusions drawn from the text.

2. Determine central ideas or themes of a text and analyze their development; summarize the key supporting details and ideas.

3. Analyze how and why individuals, events, and ideas develop and interact over the course of a text.

Craft and Structure

4. Interpret words and phrases as they are used in a text, including determining technical, connotative, and figurative meanings, and analyze how specific word choices shape meaning or tone.

5. Analyze the structure of texts, including how specific sentences, paragraphs, and larger portions of the text (e.g., a section, chapter, scene, or stanza) relate to each other and the whole.

6. Assess how point of view or purpose shapes the content and style of a text.

Integration of Knowledge and Ideas

7. Integrate and evaluate content presented in diverse formats and media, including visually and quantitatively, as well as in words.

8. Delineate and evaluate the argument and specific claims in a text, including the validity of the reasoning as well as the relevance and sufficiency of the evidence.

9. Analyze how two or more texts address similar themes or topics in order to build knowledge or to compare the approaches the authors take.

Range of Reading and Level of Text Complexity

10. Read and comprehend complex literary and informational texts independently and proficiently.

Figure 1.2. College and Career Readiness Anchor Standards for Writing

Text Types and Purposes*

1. Write arguments to support claims in an analysis of substantive topics or texts, using valid reasoning and relevant and sufficient evidence.

2. Write informative/explanatory texts to examine and convey complex ideas and information clearly and accurately through the effective selection, organization, and analysis of content.

3. Write narratives to develop real or imagined experiences or events using effective technique, well-chosen details, and well-structured event sequences.

Production and Distribution of Writing

4. Produce clear and coherent writing in which the development, organization, and style are appropriate to task, purpose, and audience.

5. Develop and strengthen writing as needed by planning, revising, editing, rewriting, or trying a new approach.

6. Use technology, including the Internet, to produce and publish writing and to interact and collaborate with others.

Research to Build and Present Knowledge

7. Conduct short as well as more sustained research projects based on focused questions, demonstrating understanding of the subject under investigation.

8. Gather relevant information from multiple print and digital sources, assess the credibility and accuracy of each source, and integrate the information while avoiding plagiarism.

9. Draw evidence from literary or informational texts to support analysis, reflection, and research.

Range of Writing

10. Write routinely over extended time frames (time for research, reflection, and revision) and shorter time frames (a single sitting or a day or two) for a range of tasks, purposes, and audiences.

Source: Common Core State Standards for English Language Arts and Literacy in History/Social Studies, Science, and Technical Subjects. © Copyright 2010. National Governors Association Center for Best Practices and Council of Chief State School Officers. All rights reserved.

689). Given the many demands that academic writing places on all students and the few opportunities many ELs have to practice as academic writers, ELs face significant challenges as they strive to become college and career ready.

With these challenges in mind, the National Clearinghouse for English Language Acquisition offers a variety of resources to help English learners reach these challenges. They include standards explicitly designed for ELs. Nearly all states have adopted English language development standards. The World-Class Instructional Design and Assessment (WIDA) Consortium released English language development standards in 2004 and further revised them in 2012. The amplified standards incorporate the features of academic language, connections to higher order thinking, and explicit connections to CCSS college- and career-readiness standards (see www.wida.us/standards/eld.aspx). Aligned to these standards is a comprehensive assessment system called ACCESS, which includes summative, placement, and screening assessments. Formative assessments are in development. The English Language Proficiency Assessment for the 21st Century Consortium (ELPA21), begun in 2012, is also developing standards for ELs and an English language proficiency assessment system, which includes summative, placement, and screening assessments (see, for example, the standards for the state of Oregon at www.ode.state.or.us/search/results/?id=36). A number of other states, including California and Texas, developed their own English language development (ELD) standards and assessments. New state ELD standards focus on more challenging content and academic literacy expectations than earlier ones and have been evaluated with a Council of Chief State School Officers (2012) framework to ensure that the standards correspond to the CCSS.

EXAMINING THE CONSTRAINTS FACED BY ENGLISH LEARNERS

In order to better contextualize the particular needs of ELs who must, at the same time, grapple with the demands of learning an additional language, negotiate the nuances of academic discourse, and master core subject matter, it is useful to describe the constraints they face in learning to write.

In describing the difficulty of composing written texts, Flower and Hayes (1980) aptly describe writers as simultaneously juggling "a number of demands being made on conscious attention" (p. 32).

For Flower and Hayes, "a writer caught in the act looks . . . like a very busy switchboard operator trying to juggle a number of demands on her attention and constraints on what she can do" (p. 33). For inexperienced writers, juggling too many constraints can cause "cognitive overload" (p. 33). While all learners face similar constraints when learning to write, the difficulties ELs face are magnified because they have to compose in a second language. Not only are they faced with cognitive, linguistic, communicative, contextual, textual, and affective constraints common to all writers, but they face additional cultural constraints unique to language learners (Frederiksen & Dominic, 1981). These constraints overlap and vary in importance as a function of learner needs and characteristics (see Figure 1.3).

Cognitive Constraints

English learners are often cognitively overloaded, especially in mainstreamed classrooms where they are held to the same performance standards as monolingual English speakers (Short & Fitzsimmons, 2007). They face the dual challenge of learning how to write while at the same time they are still developing proficiency in the English language. Both challenges exert considerable and sometimes competing demands on the cognitive system. Writing, as we know, requires considerable domain-specific knowledge. In order to write effectively, writers must not only acquire a good deal of knowledge about what to write (appropriate content and prior knowledge), but also know how to access and use this knowledge (procedural knowledge) during the composing process as well as have an awareness of why they are writing and for what audience (rhetorical knowledge) (Langer, 1986). EL writers furthermore must acquire a good deal of language-specific knowledge—knowledge that spans the breadth from selecting appropriate vocabulary (lexical knowledge) to putting words together into sentences (syntactic knowledge) in order to effectively convey meaning (semantic knowledge). Moreover, in order to engage in the knowledge-transforming processes of composing (Bereiter & Scardamalia, 1987) referred to in the CCSS, ELs first must develop a complex mental representation of the writing assignment, that is, what is being asked of them. Then they have to engage in problem analysis, that is, deciding what to say and how to say it, and finally plan how they will go about doing so. Each of these demands places a burden on a writer's working memory system, sometimes resulting in writers being "overloaded" as a result of having to juggle these multiple processes.

Figure 1.3. Juggling Constraints

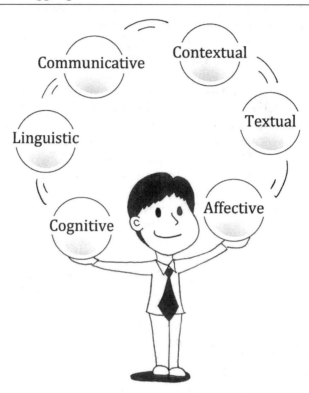

Working memory is thought to be a limited-capacity cognitive system wherein trade-offs may occur between knowledge storage and knowledge-processing demands (Baddeley & Hitch, 1974, 1994). As more resources are devoted to processing functions, fewer resources are available for storage of information. Furthermore, every increase in the cognitive load associated with one process results in a decrease in the remaining resources available for other processes. Therefore, due to the limited processing capacity of working memory, at any given time only a limited number of cognitive operations can be undertaken. The other operations must be performed automatically in order to relieve the cognitive load (Baddeley, 2003; Baddeley & Hitch, 1974,1994; Bourdin & Fayol, 1994). This idea of a limited-capacity information-processing system is especially significant for ELs since they have to simultaneously accommodate many competing demands.

EL writers experience increased demands on their working memory due to their developing second language proficiency. As a result, many ELs, as well as novice monolingual English-speaking writers, often resort to a knowledge-telling (Bereiter & Scardamalia, 1987) approach to writing, wherein they simply retell what they know about a given topic. Knowledge telling usually requires simple retrieval of information from long-term memory, unlike knowledge transforming, which additionally engages planning and revising processes that require considerably more cognitive effort (Kellogg, 2008; McCutchen, 1988). Since the working memory has a limited capacity, ELs may have to make decisions about which writing processes to prioritize when under pressure to produce text rapidly. Often, formulation (planning, translating) concerns take precedence as they are more critical and pressing than execution (handwriting/typing) and monitoring (revising, editing) processes. In fact, ELs often find translating (choosing the right words and forming them into sentences) problematic as they have limited second language resources and/or difficulty accessing these resources (Yuan & Ellis, 2003). Writing thus involves not only the language system but also the cognitive system for memory and thinking. In order to write effectively, writers must not only have a good deal of knowledge about language and writing, but also be able to rapidly retrieve such information and actively maintain it in working memory (Kellogg, 2008). This is possible only when there is sufficient working memory capacity available to maintain and manipulate multiple representations of the text, that is, when learners are able to plan and generate new text (What am I going to say next?), while at the same time reviewing content and text that have already been generated (How does this fit in with what I said before?). Because working memory is limited in capacity, such control depends on reducing the cognitive load of these acts of composing through the automatization of some of the writing processes.

Linguistic Constraints

Adding to cognitive constraints is the constraint of mastering the constellation of language knowledge necessary to successfully participate in school. When ELs write, they draw upon the sum of their language experiences. For instance, when they have to decide how to spell a word, where to place a period or an adjective, how to introduce a character, or how to organize supporting details, they utilize their linguistic resources as well as their metalinguistic awareness or conscious attention to the ways in which language is used and conveys meaning. Their linguistic resources include their knowledge of the sound system, vocabulary, morphology, syntactic rules, and semantics of the English language. They also include pragmatics, which determines when and why a specific language feature is used (Larsen-Freeman, 1991). As Zwiers, O'Hara, and Pritchard (2013) explain, "Students learn to use pieces such as facts, rules [of language], and word meanings to understand and communicate whole ideas in meaningful ways across disciplines" (p. 4).

Whereas many ELs may have good oral language proficiency, most lack the academic language proficiency necessary for success in school (Biancarosa & Snow, 2004). Consider Van Nguyen, who is representative of the Generation 1.5 group described by Roberge et al. (2009). She arrived in the United States at the age of 5 and never received English language development instruction in elementary school or secondary school. By the time she reached the University of California, Irvine, she was convinced she had acquired high proficiency in English. She had received high grades in her honors English and A.P. English courses and spoke English at home. When she was placed in a low-level ESL course at the University of California, Irvine, she wrote the following letter to her instructor:

> Dear Mrs. Robbin,
>
> I really not need humanity 20 writing class because since time I come to United State all my friend speak language. Until now everyone understand me and I dont' need study language. I don't know Vietnam language. I speak only English. I have no communication problem with my friend in dorm. My English teacher in high school key person to teach me.
>
> My teacher explained to me that how important the book was for the student and persuaded me read many book. I get A in English throughout high school and I never take ESL. I agree that some student need class but you has not made a correct decision put me in English class. Please do not makes me lose the face. I have confident in English. (Scarcella, 2003, p. 161)

Van, like our middle school student, Marisela Gonzalez, whom we introduced at the beginning of this chapter, used informal or social English even in academic settings. When using this type of English in daily conversation, it was possible for Van to communicate her thoughts without using English in a grammatically correct way. Van could be understood well without using sophisticated vocabulary, articles, prepositions, or even adding -s endings to words. She had not learned academic language, the language of school and assessments as well as the language of power. Academic language is associated with academic contexts (Scarcella, 2003; Schleppegrell, 2009). It is precisely the type of specialized knowledge that novice writers, in particular ELs like Van, are still developing.

We use the term *register* here to refer to specific features of language that vary according to the context, content, and purpose of communication. Academic registers are characterized by precision and economy of expression, logical progression of ideas, controlled sentence structure, variety in sentence structure, support for claims, conceptual/abstract treatment of topics, and adherence to the expectations of specific types of writing such as arguments. These same features of language play a key role in the CCSS that are aligned with college and work expectations. The standards call on students to use language in increasingly sophisticated and accurate ways to accomplish a range of functions, for example, formulating claims and hypotheses, synthesizing information, and developing explanations.

Understanding academic registers, which can be difficult and confusing even for monolingual English-speaking students, is especially challenging for ELs (Schleppegrell, 2009). This is because ELs like Marisela and Van receive wide exposure to everyday, informal registers of English and only restricted exposure to academic registers. Yet research shows that control of academic language is one of the key determiners of success in developing academic writing proficiency (Christie & Macken-Horarik, 2007). For recent literature on academic English, refer to Bunch (2006), Cummins and Yee-Fun (2007), and Zwiers et al. (2013).

Additionally, the acquisition of specific aspects of academic writing proficiency is constrained by factors affecting language development and the entire language acquisition process. For example, rate of language acquisition varies as a function of the degree to which ELs have been exposed to literacy and academic language; their access to continuous formal education, including writing instruction and feedback; and their ability to use their home language to read and write for academic purposes and to make meaning of the world (Ellis, 2009). Rate also is affected by the extent to which ELs pay attention to words and word parts, and learners' previous development of linguistic features.

Many teachers have ELs in their classrooms who acquired English informally by interacting with peers. When they ask such a student to write a short paragraph, the student might write:

> My name is Juan[2] an firstable I mention about my family. I come from a large famly. Becuz i have 3 brother and 4 sister and a dog. And secondable, I play sport.

2. Pseudonym.

One of the authors had such a student, and pointing to the word *firstable*, she asked him if he saw anything wrong with the word. The student said, "No!" She tried to explain that *firstable* was not a word and that the student probably intended to write the fixed expression "first of all." When the student still disagreed with her, she finally took out a dictionary and showed the student that *firstable* was not included as a word. The student told her he learned the word *firstable* in elementary school, no one had ever corrected him before, and he often had used the word before. The word had become a stable part of the student's language use. Language is learned through approximation of standard usages, and making mistakes is an integral part of language learning; however, as the student's example shows, many errors do not disappear over time without feedback. Most adolescent LTELs like Juan benefit from sustained feedback over time to improve their use of academic language.

Communicative Constraints

In addition to the constraints imposed by language and cognition, students are also subject to communicative constraints, or the constraints imposed by the need to write for a specified audience. Just as when we talk to others in face-to-face situations and we adapt our language to their communicative needs, so, too, do good writers modify their language to meet the needs of different audiences. They think about why they are writing to specific readers and what goals they want to accomplish. As Frederiksen and Dominic (1981) point out, "The degree to which a writer is aware of the need to adjust the content and expression of a message to its potential reception can influence a whole range of composing processes" (p. 3). Effective writers, then, are able to construct rich and detailed representations of the audience, which, in turn, informs their composing processes in equally rich and elaborate ways; novice writers, by contrast, create little more than "stick figure" readers (Flower, 1981, p. 65), which often results in what Flower (1979) refers to as writer-based prose. Too often, novice writers offer up their "un-retouched and under-processed" thoughts in writer-based prose that seems not to take into account the needs of the reader but rather reflects the narrative meanderings of the writer's stream-of-consciousness thought (Flower, 1979, p. 19). Such "non-communicative" prose may be a reflection of the writer's limited ability to "assume the point of view" of the reader, and thus can be quite difficult to read as ideas often are presented in the order in which they occurred to the writer rather in than some sort of hierarchical or logical manner. Reader-based prose, on the other hand, involves a deliberate attempt to communicate with the reader, by creating a "shared language" and "shared context" between the reader and writer (Flower, 1979, p. 20). In order to accomplish this, writers have to draw from their knowledge and experience and turn facts into concepts, concepts into propositions, and propositions into meaningful arguments. They have to engage in a wide range of text-based writing and conversation activities.

Many teachers have had ELs in their classrooms who send these types of email messages to them:

> Subject: Plz Rite me ASAP!!!
> From: SKATA4LIFE@xxxx.com
> Date: Fri, January 27, 2012 4:26 pm
> To: xxxx@xxusd.edu
> Hey my teacher,
> It's me. Sorry I did not turn in my wting in class today. Bad luck 4 me. I forgoted bring my binder. I now that not so gr8t. but everything was in the binder. I wuz busy morning and yesterday study chemisty test and ya know what? I went to bed almost 3:00 in the morning. I waked up at 6:30 and tried to leave at 7:30. Although I know that I must be responsble for my class but student sometiems can make mistake right? So you take my essay now!!! I attach it!!! Ple::::z respond right away!!!! Thank you my teacher and have a nice day.

Most teachers are not very happy when they receive such messages. The teachers consider them poorly edited and question the competence of the writer. Some students, fortunately for them, do not sign their names and leave their teachers wondering who sent messages with email addresses such as SKATA4LIFE.

Like their monolingual English-speaking peers, ELs are in the process of learning the linguistic features of a large number of registers, the varieties of language used for particular purposes and in specific social settings. Students who have learned only informal, everyday language may not know that they need to shift to a formal variety of English when writing email messages to instructors. Many ELs, particularly older learners who have arrived in the United States recently, may not understand the communicative needs of diverse audiences and may not be able to vary their language appropriately to meet those needs.

Contextual Constraints

Contextual constraints involve the circumstances in which writing takes place. The context or situation in which students write, including the writing assignment, the topic, the intended audience, the writer's motivation, as well as any and all relevant information, can exert a strong influence on their composing processes (Hayes & Flower, 1983). For example, are they in a timed on-demand writing situation responding to an unfamiliar prompt with high-stakes consequences? Or are they writing on a topic of their choice in a succession of drafts that will evolve over time with supportive feedback from their teacher and peers? Is the instruction they are receiving teacher-centered or student-centered (Gándara, 1997)? Do they have opportunities to collaborate with one another, or are they expected to work in isolation (Gutiérrez, 1992)? Is their audience themselves, a peer, a trusted adult, the teacher, or unknown audiences? The particular context can influence how writers decide what information is relevant, how they construct meaning, and the voice or register they adopt.

The CCSS assert that in order to be college and career ready, students must have the "flexibility, concentration, and fluency" (National Governors Association, p. 41) to produce high-quality, first-draft writing under timed conditions as well as the capacity to revise and improve multiple-draft writing over extended time frames. An additional constraint is that students are expected to negotiate these demands independently, "without significant scaffolding" (p. 7). These contextual constraints pose major challenges for ELs who may possess neither the flexibility nor the fluency to perform in these contexts.

Textual Constraints

When students are composing, they bring to the writing task knowledge of the content and the form of all prior texts they have written. Not only do expert writers have a great deal of such knowledge, but their knowledge is highly organized and conceptually integrated so that they are able to rapidly recognize familiar patterns of information. In a recent Institute of Education Sciences (IES) Practice Guide, *Teaching Elementary School Students to Be Effective Writers* (Graham et al., 2012), which includes grade 6, the expert panel had this to say about the importance of enabling students to write in a variety of genres:

Regardless of current assessment practices in a particular state, it is important for students to learn to write for varied purposes. Writing for multiple purposes encourages preparation for high-stakes assessments, even if those assessments define the purposes of writing more narrowly. In fact, writing in one genre often calls on expertise from other types of writing. Writing a persuasive essay, for example, can involve providing a narrative example, drawing a comparison, or explaining a scientific concept in order to support a point. As teachers introduce new genres of writing, they can point out writing strategies or elements of writing required for the state writing assessments. (p. 34)

Similarly, the CCR Anchor Standards for Writing call for students to be able to "combine elements of different kinds of writing—for example to use narrative strategies within argument and explanation within narrative—to produce complex and nuanced writing" (National Governors Association, 2010, p. 41).

Textual constraints are compounded for ELs, especially if the discourse features of a genre in English are different from those in the students' first language (Connor, 2008). As mentioned previously, many ELs also lack practice in the more sophisticated forms of academic writing and in the more formal registers of academic English required for success in postsecondary education.

To help ELs overcome these constraints and enhance their textual repertoire, it is important to enable them to read and write texts in a variety of text types (narrative, informative/explanatory, argument) and sub-genres (i.e., friendly letter, diary entry, recipe, newspaper article, controversial issue essay, and so forth).

Affective Constraints

As Krathwohl, Bloom, and Masia point out in their *Taxonomy of Educational Objectives: Affective Domain* (1964), nearly all cognitive objectives have an affective counterpart. These researchers liken the interdependence of the affective and cognitive domains to a man scaling a wall via two intertwining stepladders:

The ladders are so constructed that the rungs of one ladder fall between the rungs of the other. The attainment of some complex goal is made possible by alternately climbing a rung on one ladder, which brings the rung of the next ladder within reach. Thus alternating between the affective and the cognitive domains, one may seek a cognitive goal using the attainment of a cognitive goal to raise interest (an affective goal). This permits the achievement of a high cognitive goal, and so on. (p. 60)

In their research on motivation and engagement of ELs, Meltzer and Hamann (2005) note that U.S. schools are not serving even monolingual English speakers very well and that "it is essential that teachers be able to successfully motivate ELs to engage with academic texts written in English through reading, writing, and speaking" (p. 13) if we want them to develop confidence and competence. The researchers note that, like other students, most ELs disengage when they are embarrassed; when they are presented with tasks that are too far above or too far below their language proficiency, particularly if they are not in environments where they feel like they are valued members of the classroom community; and when they are not given frequent opportunities and strategies to develop as successful readers and writers, particularly if they are not in environments where they are valued members of a classroom community and if they are not given strategies to develop as successful readers and writers. Tchudi and Mitchell (1999) note that "too often the affective domain in secondary classrooms is pooh-poohed and dismissed as non-essential" (p. 118). However, students need both the skill and the will in order to succeed in school (Gambrell, Malloy, & Mazzoni, 2007). For example, in recalling her trials and tribulations as an English learner trying to acquire academic literacy in school, Hetty Jun had this to say:

> When I think of how I learned to read and write, responses such as frustration, pulling hair, blurred vision, and headaches are the things I remember. Mastering skills in reading and writing was difficult. In retrospect, I believe I have struggled with reading and writing ever since my immigration to the United States.
>
> I was reading but I did not understand the deep structure of the text . . . [and] my writing suffered as a consequence of my poor abilities in reading comprehension. Many of my answers in junior high school were superficial responses. When I tried to analyze or think critically, my head felt clogged with "stuff" . . . Oftentimes, writing was an excruciating and emotionally draining process where empty gratification awaited what seemed like my "best" efforts. I recall comments such as "awkward sentence structure," "how does this relate or support your topic?" "Are you sure this is what the author meant?" or "a better word would be . . . ." I pondered the teacher's remarks and made changes. . . . I tried to guess what she wanted from me. I was always asking, "Is this what the teacher wanted?"

I stopped this guessing game in graduate school. . . . My professor provided me with detailed constructive feedback that helped me see how to improve. I am astonished that someone in my academic life took the time to critique and highlight my writing strengths and needs, rather than attack and bleed on my paper with unclear and cryptic remarks. . . . As my writing improved, my anxiety and frustration began to subside.

I cannot say that I do cartwheels when I am asked to write a 10-page paper. But, over time and with practice, that act of reading and writing became an automatic and natural process. (Olson, 2011, p. 78. Reprinted and electronically reproduced by permission of Pearson Education, Inc., Upper Saddle River, New Jersey)

As is evident from Hetty's self-portrait (see Figure 1.4), she was juggling affective constraints, which contributed to cognitive overload. Because her teachers did not make explicit what it is that experienced readers and writers do, Hetty had to resort to guessing. She struggled to respond to those cryptic red marks and became anxious. Her anxiety, in turn, clouded her thinking, further affecting the coherence of her reading and writing. Nevertheless, Hetty did not give up. She persevered until she found an influential teacher who made visible for her what it is that expert readers and writers do, offered detailed, constructive feedback regarding how to improve her work, repeatedly provided occasions to practice, and motivated her by encouraging her and validating her efforts. Neither Hetty nor any other English learner should have to wait until graduate school for this opportunity to arise.

For many ELs who lack confidence and have low literacy self-esteem, the motivation to read and write can depend on their judgment concerning whether their teacher will give up on them or demonstrate belief that they are worth the investment of the teacher's time and encouragement (Guthrie & Wigfield, 2000; Smith & Wilhelm, 2002). ELs, in particular, need to be in safe classroom spaces where it is OK to participate, even with less-than-perfect English (Meltzer & Hamann, 2005), and where teachers provide clear expectations and supportive feedback that are appropriate for their students' level of English language proficiency.

Cultural Constraints

Students bring rich and varied cultural knowledge to the task of writing. Their cultural background should be viewed as an asset. Therefore, when teachers ignore their students' cultures, they

Figure 1.4. Hetty on Overload

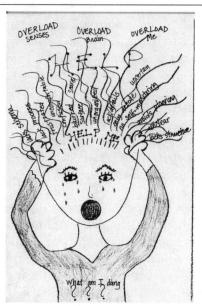

Source: Hetty Jun. Reprinted with permission.

miss valuable opportunities to connect with their students, motivate them, and enhance all students' educations (González, Moll, & Amanti, 2005). Moreover, they are unable to build their students' knowledge of the cultural information required to write effectively for diverse audiences. In some instances, students may need more information about U.S./American culture in order to achieve success as writers. For example, many young ELs, particularly those who have not lived in the United States very long, may not know how to write about trick or treating, Thanksgiving dinner, camping, or hiking, as well as many other topics. Not only will they need instruction in the vocabulary, grammar, and rhetorical features required to write about these topics, but they also will need the background knowledge and experiences. Older ELs may be even more disadvantaged, since they are expected to already have a great deal of cultural information.

Additionally, styles of narration and expository writing can vary across cultures. ELs sometimes use rhetorical features from their first languages to communicate in writing. For instance, adolescent ELs from some Asian first language backgrounds might transfer an indirect approach that they have learned in their home countries into their English compositions (Hill, 2003) by writing around a topic instead of getting directly to the point. These learners might embrace an indirect style of writing in which thesis statements are avoided, implied, or stated indirectly. Similarly, ELs from Spanish first language backgrounds might have learned an approach to writing formal introductions in which they introduce claims in elaborate ways that might seem flowery or unnecessarily verbose, at least from a U.S./American perspective. Because the CCSS emphasize the use of evidence to inform, argue, and analyze, and because the use of evidence varies across cultures, many ELs might not know what evidence to cite to support specific claims, where to put this evidence, or how to cite it. What they have learned about evidence in their home countries might affect their use of evidence in their English writing.

JUGGLING THE CONSTRAINTS

Let us return to the analytical essay that Marisela Gonzalez produced in her 6th-grade classroom and consider the constraints she was juggling as she composed this piece of writing. First and foremost, Marisela was juggling the contextual constraint of producing a complex text under timed writing conditions. She faced a textual constraint because she had had very little prior exposure to the essay genre and was unfamiliar with the conventions of academic essay writing. She also struggled with linguistic and communicative constraints because she was writing for the teacher as an evaluator and she did not have command of the register of academic English required for this essential "school" genre. Add to these three kinds of cognitive constraints that, first, her knowledge of the topic (the devastating impact of the Haiti earthquake on the Haitian people) was limited to the little she could glean from the article; and, second, that she lacked strategies to deconstruct the prompt, brainstorm ideas, plan her composition, revise under timed conditions, and edit her paper, all of which placed a cognitive strain on her working memory. As a result, she resorted to a knowledge-telling approach to her essay, essentially summarizing what happened rather than adopting a knowledge-transforming stance. Although Marisela does not share the same cultural background as the Haitian people, she did respond to their plight with sincere empathy and her essay demonstrates a great deal of effort and motivation. (Many students wrote a sentence or two in response to the prompt and then gave up.) Still, one can assume that the pressure of being asked to undertake such a difficult task under timed conditions might have caused some anxiety on her part.

INSTRUCTIONAL CONSIDERATIONS

A middle school teacher states that his students mainly come from Chinese first language backgrounds and "do not understand how thesis statements are formed." He teaches his students through contrastive analysis, comparing English and Chinese essay construction. However, most of his students were born in the United States and have never learned to write essays in Chinese.

Another middle school teacher believes that the best way to ensure that her English learners understand the literature in their textbook is to answer the literal comprehension questions about plot, setting, and character at the back of each selection and to write one-paragraph summaries describing what happened. Unfortunately, when they are asked on the high-stakes state writing assessment to read a text and write an essay interpreting the author's message, these students dutifully retell the story and receive a score of 1 out of 4 on the state rubric.

A veteran teacher of a class of 9th-graders spends nights and weekends painstakingly marking each and every error on the papers her English learners hand in. She is perplexed that not only do the students continue to make the same errors on subsequent papers but their papers seem to be getting shorter, their sentences less complex, and their ideas more superficial.

These anecdotes suggest that many teachers, often with the best of intentions, adopt practices to help their ELs improve as writers that are not always well suited to the students' needs. In fact, misunderstandings abound regarding the characteristics of "English learners," the constraints second language learners face when writing in a second language, and the practices that are most effective in helping English learners develop strong writing skills. Teachers need high-quality professional development in first and second language acquisition, reading and writing in a second language, and methods for teaching content subjects to ELs, yet this type of comprehensive and intensive curricular and pedagogical education and support is largely absent in most preservice teacher preparation programs. In their report entitled *Educating English Language Learners: Building Teacher Capacity Round Table Report* (Ballantyne, Sanderman, & Levy, 2008), found that only four states (Arizona, California, Florida, and New York) require teachers to have specific coursework or separate certification for teaching ELs, with as many as 15 states requiring no preservice EL-specific preparation. The remaining states make some reference to language diversity and/or meeting the special needs of ELs in their certification standards, but there is great variation in what preparation is required. As Goldenberg (2013) suggests, "It is an inconvenient truth that we lack the knowledge base to fully prepare teachers to help many of their ELs overcome the achievement gaps they face" (p. 11).

Let's take a look at what Maria Gómez-Greenberg would need to know in order to help Marisela Gonzalez improve her composition. Ms. Gómez-Greenberg is a second language learner herself. Having immigrated to the United States from Colombia when she was 13, she has a special empathy for her students' struggles with academic English. Also, as a native-Spanish speaker, she can take advantage of her knowledge of cognates, or words that look similar in Spanish and English, as well as her own earlier challenges in learning English, to help her students understand the meaning of many English words. However, as a student, Ms. Gómez-Greenberg received little instruction in how to write academic essays in English herself. She further possesses limited preparation in how to teach her students to master the formal register of English and genre conventions of the interpretive text-based essay that are so often the gateway to postsecondary success. As a consequence, she is concerned with how best to address the challenges presented in her students' essays.

When Ms. Gómez-Greenberg read Marisela's essay, she realized that Marisela had little understanding of how to structure a formal essay. For example, her essay lacked a lead-in sentence, a thesis statement, and supporting details. Instead, Marisela conjoined her ideas into one long paragraph. As a result of her diagnostic assessment, Ms. Gómez-Greenberg knew that she had to teach Marisela how to write a formal introduction with a thesis, a main body, and a conclusion. Beyond the form of the academic essay was the issue of idea generation. She pondered how to move Marisela beyond knowledge telling to get her to actually analyze and comment upon the theme of Leonard Pitts's article. She also noticed that Marisela had to expand her meta-knowledge about writing for a formal audience. Marisela used conversational English to write her essay. In formal essays, a different register of English is expected by the reader. For example, instead of "donate stuff like close [sic]," we might say, "donate articles of clothing." But how could she help Marisela write in this academic register without simply rewriting the phrases for her? Finally, Ms. Gómez-Greenberg realized that she needed to develop a plan for how to tackle Marisela's numerous spelling errors. She chose one spelling pattern in particular—the understanding that past tense spelling often requires an "e" before a "d"—and she taught a mini lesson to Marisela and others in the class who displayed the same lack of orthographic knowledge. But what to address next? Ms. Gómez-Greenberg's assessment of Marisela's writing brought to light her own need to acquire more skills and strategies in order to benefit her students (Fitzgerald et al., 2014).

CONNECTING READING AND WRITING
TO MEET THE COMMON CORE STATE STANDARDS

The purpose of this book is to provide teachers like Maria Gómez-Greenberg with the knowledge, pedagogical tools, and curricular resources needed to help reduce the constraints faced by ELs as they engage in academic writing and to prepare them to meet the Common Core State Standards. Although the focus of the book is on how to facilitate the development of ELs' writing ability in secondary school, with a special emphasis on the CCR Anchor Standards for Writing in the text types showcased in the CCSS—argument, informative/explanatory, and narrative—substantial attention also will be paid to the CCR Anchor Standards for Reading. Given the strong emphasis on text-based analytical writing in the CCSS, it is essential to connect reading and writing. Research indicates that using writing as a learning tool in reading instruction leads to better reading achievement, and that using reading as a resource for elaborating on ideas or for understanding opposing views leads to better writing performance (Graham & Hebert, 2010; Tierney & Shanahan, 1991; Tierney, Soter, O'Flahavan, & McGinley 1989). Further, research suggests that "reading and writing in combination have the potential to contribute in powerful ways to thinking" (Tierney et al., 1989, p. 166). Hence, the integration of reading and writing instruction contributes to cultivating the kind of "open-minded but discerning" critical thinkers called for in the CCSS (p. 7). Since listening and speaking are also essential skills for the language acquisition of ELs, these standards as well as the language standards will be addressed.

Recognizing the need to develop her own expertise in order to enhance the academic literacy of her students, Ms. Gómez-Greenberg volunteered to participate in a 2-year professional development program focused on how to prepare ELs to meet the Common Core State Standards. Using many of the strategies, activities, and lessons in this book, she helped her students to transition from performing at a below basic level to becoming more proficient academic writers. Seven months after Marisela wrote her timed essay on "Sometimes, the Earth Is Cruel" by Leonard Pitts, she wrote the following timed essay analyzing "The Man in the Water" by Roger Rosenblatt (1982):

Are you willing to risk your life to save someone else? "The Man in the Water," by Roger Rosenblatt, is a nonfiction story about a man who died to save strangers. My theme is to try to save as many people as you can. On January 13, 1982, Air Florida Flight 90 crashed into a river. Then, the plane hit seven vehicles, killing four motorists and 74 passengers. Well there is good news 6 passengers got to survive in this airplane crash. Let me tell you readers there was one passenger from the plane that was very brave. He saved 6 people life. They didn't know his name but he had an extravagant mustache. A park police helicopter team lowered a rope, but the man let those 6 people to go before him. "In a mass casualty, you'll find people like him." I can't believe how brave this man was and that he was a stranger to the other passengers.

The author uses lots of good language to describe the accident. Like one of them he uses the simile "like famished gulls" describing how the planes swoop in the sky. And the Air Florida plane is like "a flying garden" that is destroyed by the icy water. Rosenblatt feels so proud of our hero because he saved as much people as he could. He gave a lifeline not just to the people but to us. This means that we have hope. The article taught me to always try to save as many people as you can. The message is that if a regular guy can do this for strangers then we could do it to.

While some issues linger, it is clear that Marisela's writing is much improved.

In the following chapters of this book, we will share research-based pedagogical strategies, activities, and full-length lessons designed to help ELs in English language arts classrooms become more confident and competent readers and writers who meet the rigorous Common Core State Standards necessary to become college and career ready. Although the CCSS privilege argument writing by listing the writing types in order from argument to informative/explanatory, and finally narrative, we purposely are reversing the order in this book because we believe not only that focusing on narrative reduces the constraints on student writers (since their narratives often deal with familiar content, such as personal memories), but also that narrative writing builds fundamental writing skills that can be used to enhance other types of writing. Throughout the book, we will provide glimpses into the classrooms of exemplary and dedicated teachers like Maria Gómez-Greenberg to highlight their best practices and share samples of their EL students' writing. We will include curricular activities geared for students at the developing-to-advanced levels of English proficiency. Additionally, we will indicate how these activities will help ELs overcome the various constraints they face as writers. We hope that our book will help teachers enable ELs to internalize these best practices and, ultimately, perform complex reading and writing tasks independently.

To Sum Up

- ELs are a diverse group of learners with unique experiences and needs.
- They face the multiple challenges of, at the same time, acquiring a new language, mastering core subject matter, and negotiating the nuances of academic discourse.
- ELs must simultaneously juggle multiple demands on their working memory, including cognitive, linguistic, communicative, contextual, textual, affective, and cultural constraints.
- The CCSS set a high bar for student achievement with their emphasis on analyzing and interpreting challenging texts and using academic discourse in extended pieces of writing, which may be compounded for EL students given the many additional constraints they face.
- Much of the responsibility for EL students' learning and success rests on the shoulders of teachers who themselves are often ill-prepared to meet their students' needs.
- Teachers need high-quality preservice and inservice professional development in methods for teaching reading and writing to non-native speakers of English.

CHAPTER 2

Best Practices for Teaching Writing to English Learners

How can English learners who are developing their proficiency in academic language navigate the challenging writing tasks advocated in the Common Core State Standards by themselves? The language demands of writing and the many constraints ELs must juggle while composing are such that ELs require instructional assistance to convey ideas and information, construct viable arguments, and critique the arguments of others in cohesive, well-reasoned written texts. As Goldenberg (2013) reminds us, "It should be clear that despite progress in understanding how to improve teaching and learning for the millions of ELs in our schools, many gaps remain. The challenges posed by the Common Core State Standards make those gaps more glaring" (p. 10). We look first to what research can tell us about effective practices to enhance the academic literacy of ELs.

RESEARCH ON WRITING INSTRUCTION FOR ENGLISH LEARNERS

Multiple books, articles, and policy reports on grades 6–12 EL writing instruction have been written in the past 10 years (for a recent summary, see Ferris & Hedgcock, 2013). Much has been written on the development of second language writing studies as a field of practice (Matsuda & Silva, 2005), critical pedagogy in L2 writing (Pennycook, 2001), biliteracy (Hornberger, 1989), literacy in different modalities (New London Group, 1996), digital literacy (Warschauer, 2009), sociocultural theories on the particular kinds of literacy that are valued in different settings (Gee, 2011; Gutiérrez, Morales, & Martinez, 2009; Street, 2005), intercultural rhetoric (Connor, 2011), basic research on writers and their composing processes (Polio & Williams, 2009), particular groups of writers such as Generation 1.5 students and their needs (Harklau et al., 1999), linguistic features of writing and their development (Ortega, 2003), and error analysis (Ferris, 2011).

Despite the explosion of publications, the dearth of empirical studies on effective practices for teaching writing to ELs reveals that this research area is nearly untapped (August & Shanahan, 2006). Most of the studies are small in size and qualitative in nature. Fitzgerald and Amendum (2007), for example, report no empirical studies of grades 6–12 writing instruction in their meta-analysis that involved 1988–2003 research studies of the K–12 writing instruction for ELs in the United States. Panofsky et al. (2005) summarize the available research and point out the growing need to investigate effective practices for teaching writing to adolescent ELs. This lack of research leaves teachers of the over 1 million EL students largely to speculate about how best to teach their students. How can they teach students to meet the rigorous standards of the CCSS when they have had so little training in how to diversify instruction in order to meet the needs of the entire spectrum of ELs, from newcomers to LTELs? Fortunately, despite the scarcity of scientific studies on writing instruction of ELs in grades 6–12, promising research-based practices are beginning to emerge indicating that ELs need types of high-quality writing instruction similar to what adolescents who speak only English need, as well as additional supports. Goldenberg (2013) explains that existing studies suggest that what is known about effective instruction ought to be the foundation of effective teaching for English learners. Drawing on the research, he argues that, in general, ELs benefit from clear instructions and supportive guidance as they engage with new skills; effective modeling of skills, strategies, and procedures; active student engagement and participation; effective feedback; applying new learning and transferring this learning to new situations; practice and periodic review; structured, focused interactions with other students; regular assessments, with reteaching as needed; and well-established classroom routines and behavior norms. He notes that in all the research he reviewed, students made significant progress, improving their English if "at least several of these practices were incorporated into their instruction" (p. 5).

BEST PRACTICES FOR TEACHING WRITING TO ENGLISH LEARNERS

What follows are best practices that research has shown benefit ELs as they develop academic literacy. First and foremost, designing and implementing culturally responsive curricula and instruction is fundamental to effective practice and has gained much traction in recent years, as has an emphasis on understanding student motivation and reducing the affective barriers that may block learning (Meltzer & Hamann, 2005). Strategy instruction also has been widely accepted as one of the most effective practices for literacy development, not only for ELs but for all students (Graham & Perin, 2007). Additionally, modeling appropriate language use and processes of connecting reading and writing is important, as is scaffolding instruction using graphic organizers and meaningful visuals to support student learning. And finally, it is generally accepted that ELs need explicit instruction in academic English, opportunities to practice and develop this complex register of language, and formative assessment to monitor progress and craft ongoing instruction (Gersten, Baker, Shanahan, Linan-Thompson, & Collins, 2007).

CREATING CULTURALLY RELEVANT WRITING INSTRUCTION IN A COMMUNITY OF LEARNERS

Despite the paucity of scientific study, there is widespread consensus that culturally relevant instruction facilitates learning, improving the access ELs have to high-quality instruction (Gutiérrez & Vossoughi, 2010). Practices that facilitate connections between students and their classrooms, homes, and communities form the basis for culturally relevant teaching and can tap particularly into the strengths that ELs bring with them to school (Goldenberg, 2012).

Diaz, Moll, and Mehan (1986) were among the first to advocate instructional approaches that built upon the unique cultural heritages of students. They found that instruction was more successful when teachers systematically drew upon students' "funds of knowledge" in designing curricula. Villegas and Lucas (2002) further suggest many culturally relevant activities that can be effective in the writing classroom, for example, involving students in discussions, building on students' interests, building on students' linguistic resources, utilizing community and home resources, helping students examine the curriculum from multiple perspectives, using examples and analogies from students' lives and communities, establishing a classroom climate that prevents bullying and discrimination, and fostering constructive relationships with parents and community members.

A growing number of researchers recognize the affective and motivational dimensions of academic literacy, asserting that there is a social as well as a cognitive dimension of literacy (Greenleaf, Schoenbach, Cziko, & Mueller, 2001). Based on their review of adolescent literacy research in general, as well as research on the literacy of adolescent ELs in particular, Meltzer and Hamann (2005) recommend three primary instructional practices to reduce the affective constraints for ELs: (1) making connections to students' lives, thereby connecting their background knowledge to the content they are learning in school; (2) creating responsive classrooms that acknowledge students' voices, giving them an element of choice in learning tasks, and strengthening their literacy skills (Valdés, 2001); and (3) engaging students in collaboration where they interact with one another about texts they are reading and writing.

One way to motivate ELs to write well is to establish a supportive environment in the classroom and create a community of writers. In *Beyond Discipline* (1996) Alfie Kohn writes:

> In saying that a classroom or school is a "community," then I mean that it is a place in which students feel cared about and are encouraged to care about each other. They experience a sense of being valued and respected; the children matter to one another and to the teacher. They have come to think in the plural: they feel connected to each other; they are part of an "us." And as a result of all this, they feel safe in their classes, not only physically but emotionally. (p. 101)

In such classrooms teachers actively encourage students to collaborate; they provide ongoing opportunities and thoughtful activities that invite students to engage in shared inquiry, keeping in mind that "what a child can do in cooperation today, he can do alone tomorrow" (Vygotsky, 1934/1986, p. 188). Building a classroom community also involves collaboration between teacher and students and lets students develop a sense of ownership in the learning.

Celebrating students' writing by displaying it in the classroom can help students feel valued. Two activities that can result in classroom displays that foster a sense of community are the My Name activity and the Biopoem.

My Name Activity

Writing about names in secondary school can be especially effective because it can "save students from feeling unimportant or not valued when no one knows their names" (Tchudi & Mitchell, 1999, p. 122). Sandra Cisneros's vignette "My Name" from *The House on Mango Street* (2013) works particularly well with English learners because the speaker, Esperanza, struggles with how her name is pronounced in English "as if the syllables were made out of tin and hurt the roof of your mouth" rather than the softer sounds "like silver" of her name in Spanish.

After reading "My Name," discussing how Esperanza feels about her name, and noticing how Esperanza compares her name to a song, an object, a color, and so on, students can fill out a sentence frame, like the ones below, comparing Esperanza's name to other things:

> If Esperanza were an animal, she would be a chameleon because she's looking for a name to change and match her mood.

> If Esperanza were a plant, she would be a dandelion because she sometimes wants to let go and fly away from her sad name.

Subsequently, students can create sentence frames about their names and a coat of arms for themselves like the one by Mathew Loayza, an EL student in Maureen Rippee's high school English language arts class, shown in Figure 2.1. Using their coats of arms as a planning strategy, students can then write paragraphs about their names that can be posted along with their illustrations. To make the task more accessible for students with less fluency in English, the teacher may want to provide a paragraph frame like the one in Figure 2.2.

Biopoem Activity

The Biopoem frequently is used by teachers as an initial writing and get-acquainted activity that creates a sense of group cohesion. Because this is a pattern poem, it offers ELs a low-risk opportunity to participate in the community. The poetry frame in Figure 2.3 is bookended by the students' first and last names and enables them to share personal information about themselves that reveals who they are and what they care about. Students' poems can be read to partners or in small groups and then decorated and displayed on a class bulletin board along with their photographs. Later, when the class is studying a work of literature, students can write a Biopoem in the voice of a literary character or a historical figure as in Figure

Figure 2.1. Coat of Arms

Mathew Loayza (student)

Coat of Arms

If my name were an animal, it would be <u>sloth</u> because <u>I am very le-</u><u>thargic</u>.

If my name were a plant, it would be <u>maple tree</u> because <u>of my reminis-</u><u>cence of childhood in Canada</u>.

If my name were a song it would be <u>immigrant song</u> because <u>of how the</u><u>song describes the distant lands like all the unknown that I fear</u>.

Source: Mathew Loayza, 2014. Reprinted with permission.

Figure 2.2. "My Name" Paragraph Frame

My parents named me _____ because _____. In the baby book, my name means _____. If my name were an animal, it would be _____ because _____. If my name were a plant, it would be a _____ because _____. When I think about my name, I feel _____.

Sample:

My parents named me Carol because I was born on Christmas Day and they thought of a story by Charles Dickens called "A Christmas Carol." In the baby book, my name means song of joy. If my name were an animal, it would be a cat because I'm very affectionate and I love to curl up in a ball and sleep. If my name were a plant, I'd be a sunflower because I have a sunny disposition. When I think about my name, I feel happy because my name is so full of cheer.

2.3. This is an example of how a teacher might help ELs make connections to their personal lives and to one another, acknowledge students' voices, and engage students in interacting with one another as readers and writers.

In their IES Practice Guide, Graham et al. (2012) base their evidence for recommending that teachers create an engaged community of writers on five intervention studies that led to positive effects on the quality of student writing. In describing the support for this recommendation, they point out that since writing is a lifelong skill and requires effort for even experienced writers, it is especially important to establish a nurturing environment in which "every member of the community has room to grow and it is acceptable to take risks and make mistakes" (p. 50).

STRATEGY INSTRUCTION

Numerous reports from policy centers and blue-ribbon panels "implicate poor understandings of cognitive strategies as the primary reason why adolescents struggle with reading and writing" (Deshler, Palinscar, Biancarosa, & Nair, as cited in Conley, 2008, p. 84; Graham, 2006; Snow & Biancarosa, 2003). According to a recent Carnegie Corporation report, inadequate educator capacity and the limited use of research-based instructional practices prevent adolescent ELs from learning academic English and meeting content standards in English language arts (Short & Fitzsimmons, 2007). To address the needs of adolescent ELs, the report encouraged teachers to help ELs use cognitive strategies to understand, interpret, and write essays about complex texts.

A number of instructional frameworks and recommendations support approaches that incorporate strategy instruction to advance ELs' development of English (Francis, Rivera, Lesaux, Keiffer, & Rivera, 2006; Goldenberg, 2008; Schleppegrell, 2009). Grounded in studies that demonstrate the efficacy of cognitive strategy use in reading and writing (Block & Pressley, 2002; Duke & Pearson, 2002; Graham & Perin, 2007; National Institute of Child Health and Development, 2000; Paris, Wasik, & Turner, 1991; Tierney & Pearson, 1983; Tierney & Shanahan, 1991), the frameworks stress the importance of including modeling, scaffolding, guided practice, and independent use of strategies so that students develop the ability to select and implement appropriate strategies independently and to monitor and regulate their use (Block & Pressley, 2002).

Short and Fitzsimmons (2007) hypothesize that strategy instruction develops ELs' English by providing them with an explicit

Figure 2.3. Biopoem

(First name)
(Four adjectives that describe the person)
Son or Daughter of (your parents' names)
Lover of (three different things that the person loves)
Who feels (three different feelings *and* when or where they are felt)
Who gives (three different things the person gives)
Who fears (three different fears the person has)
Who would like to see (three different things the person would like to
see)
Who lives (a brief description of where the person lives)
(Last name)

Barack
Strong, determined, compassionate, calm
Son of Ann Dunham and Barack Obama, Sr.
Who loves his family, books, and the Chicago Bulls
Who feels proud of his country, happy when he's with his children,
and sad when people suffer
Who gives his time, his money, and his skill to help people
Who fears discrimination, war, and lack of progress
Who would like to see all young people graduate from college
Who lives in the White House
Obama

focus on language, increasing their exposure to academic texts, making the texts they read comprehensible, giving them multiple opportunities to affirm or correct their understanding and use of language, assisting them in retrieving new language features and in using these features for academic purposes, and providing them with the means of learning language on their own, outside of class. They further hypothesize that adolescent ELs of an intermediate level of English proficiency and above have sufficient proficiency to benefit from strategy instruction (Echevarría, Vogt, & Short, 2012; Short & Fitzsimmons, 2007). These students have automatized lower level reading and writing skills. Furthermore, they possess the language proficiency required to use cognitive strategies that will provide them access to the higher order cognitive reading and writing tasks that they will encounter when they have mainstreamed into regular content instruction.

Although the Common Core State Standards do not explicitly define "the full range of metacognitive strategies that students may need to monitor and direct their learning" (p. 4) or the "the full range of support necessary for English language learners" (p. 6), teachers clearly will need to implement pedagogical strategies to help their ELs to become strategic readers and writers. Teaching struggling writers strategies for planning, in particular, has a strong impact on their writing performance (Graham, 2006).

Let's look at two pedagogical strategies, the Easy as 1, 2, 3! activity to motivate reluctant readers and the Do/What activity to help struggling writers respond appropriately to a writing prompt.

Easy as 1, 2, 3! Activity

When asked to read independently, inexperienced readers can be quick to abandon a text when they encounter unfamiliar words or a complicated story line. Donna Moore, an ELD teacher at the intermediate school level, developed a strategy called Easy as 1, 2, 3! to spark students' curiosity, to acquaint them with the text, and to build personal investment, in order to make her students less likely to tell themselves "I can't" or "I won't" and more willing to read further.

The first step in Easy as 1, 2, 3! is to prompt students to tap prior knowledge and make predictions by asking them to think about the title of a text in light of their own background knowledge and experiences and to write down and then discuss their predictions of what the text will be about based on the title. For example, in responding to Ray Bradbury's short story, "All Summer in a Day" (1998), students often predict that the story will focus on all the exciting events of summer crammed into just one short day. The next step is to select a significant picture that accompanies the text or to take a picture walk through the text and to "read" the pictures by visualizing. Students then record their predictions about the context of the text based on the pictures they have analyzed; students also are prompted to revise meaning. These thoughts are recorded on the Easy as 1, 2, 3! sheet before the class discusses them in pairs or as a whole group. In "All Summer in a Day," for instance, the picture by Robert Vickrey that a publisher selected to accompany the text creates a mood of isolation and entrapment. Students are quick to "read" the somber expression on the child's face, revise their original prediction of a fun-filled adventure, and anticipate a much gloomier outcome than they initially had expected. Finally, the teacher reads a selection from the text, if possible stopping at a spot that leaves the students in suspense. Students jot down their new or revised predictions based on how they perceived the words and then turn to a partner or to the whole class to compare their speculations. Figure 2.4 shows a graphic organizer for the Easy as 1, 2, 3! activity.

The Easy as 1, 2, 3! activity is designed to convince students that interacting with a text is as easy as making predictions about the title, "reading" the pictures through visualization, and responding

Figure 2.4. Easy as 1, 2, 3!

<table>
<tr><td align="center">

Easy as 1, 2, 3!

What Do You Know About This Story

</td></tr>
<tr><td>

(1)   This is what I think I know because of the
Title

</td></tr>
<tr><td>

(2)   This is what I think I know because of the
Pictures

</td></tr>
<tr><td>

(3)   This is what I know because of the
Words

</td></tr>
</table>

From Donna Moore, ELD Teacher, Fitz Intermediate, Garden Grove, CA.

Source: Adapted from Donna Moore, ELD Teacher, Fitz Intermediate, Garden Grove, CA.

to the words. While she's getting her students hooked and ready to read on, Moore also is fostering the cognitive strategies she wants her students to access and practice.

Do/What Activity

Students often fail to respond to a writing prompt adequately because they haven't taken the time to thoroughly examine what they are being asked to do and to plan before they start composing. Further, many struggling students and ELs who have limited practice may fall back on retelling or summarizing instead of presenting the high-level interpretation of substantive topics and texts called for in the CCSS. Teaching students to analyze the prompt and construct a Do/What chart can enable them to develop a road map for composing.

Teachers will need to model how to construct a Do/What chart with students before the students can construct one independently. For example, teachers can provide students with a prompt such as the one presented to Marisela Gonzalez, whom we met in Chapter 1, on analyzing the theme in "Sometimes, the Earth Is Cruel," an article about the Haiti earthquake, as shown in Figure 2.5. They can guide students through the prompt and demonstrate how to circle verbs that describe what the student needs to *do* in the prompt and then underline the words that indicate *what* the task is. For example, under Writing Directions, the first verb that tells the writer to do something is "select" and the task words identifying what to select are "one important theme."

Note that teachers should not take for granted that EL students understand what the verbs in the CCSS Anchor Standards, such as *analyze, make inferences, cite, support, integrate, identify, determine, reflect,* etc., mean and should realize that they will need to model the acts of mind or actions the verbs entail. Once students have circled and underlined the key words, they construct a Do/What chart beneath the prompt. Not only will this strategy help students with planning and goal setting, but, as they compose, students can refer continually to this road map to ensure that they are on course and addressing all of the elements of the prompt. In fact, in a large-scale randomized field trial of an intervention using a cognitive strategies approach to enhancing the text-based analytical writing of ELs, students who employed the Do/What chart wrote significantly higher quality essays in a timed writing situation without guidance from the teacher (Kim et al., 2011; Olson et al., 2012).

Figure 2.5. Do/What Chart

"Sometimes, the Earth Is Cruel"

Writing Situation

Two days after the Haiti earthquake on January 12, 2010, Leonard Pitts, an award-winning journalist, wrote an article for the *Miami Herald* in which he described the Haitian people's response to the tragedy which struck their country.

Writing Directions

After reading "Sometimes, the Earth Is Cruel," (select) one important theme to (write) an essay about. (Create) a theme statement which (expresses) the author's main point, lesson, or message in the article. Your theme statement will be the thesis of your essay—the claim you make about the writer's message or main idea.

As you (develop) your essay, (pay) specific attention to:

- Pitts's description of the Haitian people's actions after the earthquake
- The language Pitts uses to describe nature and the relationship between the Haitian people and nature (including similes, metaphors, symbols, personification, or other figurative language)
- Pitts's response to the way the Haitian people deal with their tragedy

When a journalist's purpose is strictly to inform, he or she will present the facts objectively without trying to influence the reader. However, Pitts does more than this. (Discuss) Pitts's purpose in writing "Sometimes, the Earth Is Cruel." What message does he want his readers to take away from reading his article and why is it especially significant?

CONNECTING READING AND WRITING THROUGH STRATEGY INSTRUCTION

In his analysis of the Common Core State Standards from his perspective as a member of the review panel for the College and Career Ready Standards for English Language Arts and of the Validation Committee that provided oversight for the development process, Arthur Applebee (2013) identifies the connection between reading and writing as one of the document's major strengths. He writes:

Figure 2.5. Do/What Chart (continued)

DO	WHAT
Select	one important theme
Write	an essay
Create	a theme statement
Express	the author's main point, lesson, or message
Develop	your essay
Pay	specific attention to: • Pitts' description • The language Pitts uses • Pitts' response • Pitts' purpose
(Answer/Discuss)	what message he wants readers to take away why the message is especially significant

The high stakes testing environment created by No Child Left Behind has privileged reading as an essential element of the English language arts curriculum, leaving writing instruction at risk. CCSS, on the other hand, elevates writing to a central place, not only giving it the same number of individual standards as reading but also making writing the central way in which content knowledge is developed and shared. (p. 27)

Indeed, the first College and Career Readiness Anchor Standard for Reading in grades 6–12 identifies writing as the key vehicle for text-based analysis:

Read closely to determine what the text says explicitly and to make logical inferences from it; cite specific textual evidence when writing or speaking to support conclusions drawn from the text. (National Governors Association, 2010, p. 35)

Reading and writing traditionally have been thought of and taught as flip sides of a coin—as opposites; "readers decoded or deciphered language and writers encoded or produced written text" (Tompkins, 2013, p. 46). However, researchers increasingly have noted the connections between reading and writing, identifying them as complementary processes of meaning construction involving the use of similar cognitive strategies (Tierney & Pearson, 1983). Strategy instruction is an especially effective way to connect reading and writing. According to Fitzgerald and Shanahan (2000), readers and writers share four basic types of knowledge: meta-knowledge about the processes of reading and writing; domain knowledge that the reader or writer brings to the text; knowledge about text attributes; and procedural knowledge and skill to negotiate reading and writing. It is precisely because reading and writing access similar cognitive strategies, but to differing degrees, that reading and writing make such a powerful combination when taught in connection with each other. Research suggests that using writing as a learning tool in reading instruction leads to better reading achievement (Graham & Hebert, 2010; Tierney & Shanahan, 1991) and that using reading as a resource for elaborating on ideas or for understanding opposing views leads to better writing performance (Tierney & Shanahan, 1991; Tierney et al., 1989). More important, reading and writing taught together engages students in a greater use and variety of cognitive strategies than does reading and writing taught separately (Tierney & Shanahan, 1991, p. 272). This exposure to and practice in an array of cognitive strategies promote and enhance critical thinking. In fact, research indicates that "reading and writing in combination have the potential to contribute in powerful ways to thinking" (Tierney et al., 1989, p. 166). This is why in analyzing principles for building an EL-responsive learning environment, Coady et al. (2003) conclude that ELs are most successful when teachers explicitly model the reading, writing, and thinking skills ELs need to master in order to function successfully in educational settings.

One way to connect reading and writing through strategy instruction is to provide students with cognitive strategy bookmarks with sentence starters that they can use to annotate the texts they are reading. Once students become adept at implementing these strategies, they can participate in book clubs where they can write letters about their texts, engage in discussions, and share artifacts they have created.

Cognitive Strategy Bookmark Activity

Prior to introducing ELs to the cognitive strategy bookmarks, the teacher will need to introduce the concept of a cognitive strategy to the class. To make this accessible, the teacher might say the following:

> Today we are going to learn about what experienced readers and writers do when they make meaning out of words. They use something called cognitive strategies to help them understand. The term *cognitive strategies* sounds very complex. Let's break it down. "Cognitive" means knowing or thinking and "strategies" are tools or tactics people use to solve a problem. So, a cognitive strategy is a thinking tool. Inside your head, you have a lot of cognitive strategies or thinking tools that you use to make sense of what you read and write. It's almost like there's a little voice inside your head that talks to you while you're reading and writing. It tells you when you're confused or when you suddenly understand something. It helps you to make pictures in your head or to decide to go back and reread something before going forward. (Olson, 2011, p. 22)

The teacher can then pass out the bookmarks in Figure 2.6 and demonstrate how to apply cognitive strategies to construct meaning by thinking aloud while reading and annotating a text.

Think-Aloud Activities

In his book *Improving Comprehension with Think-Aloud Strategies,* Jeff Wilhelm (2001) describes the following procedure for implementing think-alouds in the classroom:

Step 1: Choose a short selection of text (or a short text) that will be interesting, challenging, and could present some difficulty to students if read independently.

Step 2: Decide on a few strategies to highlight and explain to students what a think-aloud is, why you are modeling these particular strategies, and how these strategies will be helpful to them.

Step 3: State your purpose for reading the specific selection and ask students to pay attention to the strategies you select so they can explain what, why, how, and when you used them.

Step 4: Read the text aloud to students and think-aloud as you do so.

Step 5: Have students underline the words and phrases that helped you use a strategy.

Step 6: Ask them to make a list of the strategies you used and the verbal cues that prompted strategy use.

Figure 2.6. Cognitive Strategy Bookmarks

Cognitive Strategies Sentence Starters

Planning and Goal Setting
- My purpose is...
- My top priority is ...
- I will accomplish my goal by...

Tapping Prior Knowledge
- I already know that...
- This reminds me of...
- This relates to...

Asking Questions
- I wonder why...
- What if...
- How come...

Making Predictions
- I'll bet that...
- I think...
- If _____, then...

Visualizing
- I can picture...
- In my mind I see...
- If this were a movie...

Making Connections
- This reminds me of...
- I experienced this once when...
- I can relate to this because...

Summarizing
- The basic gist is...
- The key information is...
- In a nutshell, this says that..

Adopting an Alignment
- The character I most identify with is...
- I really got into the story when...
- I can relate to this author because...

Cognitive Strategies Sentence Starters

Forming Interpretations
- What this means to me is...
- I think this represents...
- The idea I'm getting is...

Monitoring
- I got lost here because...
- I need to reread the part where...
- I know I'm on the right track because ...

Clarifying
- To understand better, I need to know more about...
- Something that is still not clear is...
- I'm guessing that this means ____, but I need to...

Revising Meaning
- At first I thought ____, but now I.....
- My latest thought about this is...
- I'm getting a different picture here because...

Analyzing the Author's Craft
- A golden line for me is...
- This word/phrase stands out for me because...
- I like how the author uses _____ to show...

Reflecting and Relating
- So, the big idea is...
- A conclusion I'm drawing is...
- This is relevant to my life because...

Evaluating
- I like/don't like _____ because...
- My opinion is _____ because...
- The most important message is _____because...

For example, consider the following opening passage from Leonard Pitts's (2010) article, "Sometimes, the Earth Is Cruel":

Sometimes, the earth is cruel. That is ultimately the fundamental lesson here, as children wail, families sleep out of doors, and the dead lie unclaimed in the rubble that once was Port-au-Prince, Haiti. Sometimes the rains fall and will not stop. Sometimes the skies turn barren and will not rain. Sometimes the seas rise and smack the shoreline like a fist. Sometimes the wind bullies the land. And sometimes, the land rattles and heaves and splits itself in two. Sometimes, the earth is cruel.

After reading this passage, the teacher might say the following and then model annotating the passage:

Teacher's Think-Aloud

Okay, from reading the passage so far, I know the article is about Haiti and I have some prior knowledge that there was a devastating earthquake there a few years ago. When the author talks about children wailing and the dead lying in the rubble, which is broken stones from crumbled buildings, it reminds me of watching the TV coverage of the disaster. So, I remember that and can make a personal connection. I can really visualize how destructive the earthquake was because of the concrete details the author uses to describe the devastation in the capital city, Port-au-Prince. The author says the earth is cruel, so he's giving it personal emotions. That's called personification. For instance, he says, "the wind bullies the land," turning the wind into an enemy and the land into a victim. When he says that "the seas rise and smack the shoreline like a fist" I feel like the earth is beating up Haiti. I can really picture the fist and feel the punch because of the simile "like a fist." The way the author crafts his language is very powerful. He also repeats the word "sometimes" over and over, and it gives me the feeling that one disaster after another strikes this poor country. I'll bet that the lesson that Pitts refers to will have more to it than just that nature is cruel. But I'll have to keep reading to find out more.

As the teacher thinks aloud, he or she can annotate the text in the margins using the sentence starters such as *I already know that, I can picture, I'll bet that, The idea I'm getting is*, and so forth. The annotations also can be labeled with abbreviations such as TPK for tapping prior knowledge, MC for making connections, and so forth. Students will then need to practice using their bookmarks to annotate the text along with the teacher as a whole group before using the bookmarks independently.

Book Club Activities

Another way to connect reading and writing and promote strategy use is to engage EL students in reading, discussing, and writing about self-selected fiction and nonfiction material in book clubs. Researcher Stephen Krashen (1993) identifies free voluntary reading as "one of the most powerful tools" in language arts instruction. He writes:

> My conclusions are simple. When children read for pleasure, when they get "hooked on books," they acquire, involuntarily and without conscious effort, nearly all of the so-called "language skills" many people are so concerned about. They will become adequate readers, acquire a large vocabulary, develop a good writing style, and become good (but not necessarily perfect) spellers. . . . Without it, I suspect that children simply do not have a chance. (p. 84)

While we remain skeptical of ELs' ability to acquire *most* of the language needed to write academic texts through pleasure reading alone, we note that the preponderance of second language research makes it clear that pleasure reading plays a critical role in English language development (Ortega, 2009). Research also suggests that students who engage in frequent discussions about their reading are more motivated, have higher reading achievement, read more widely, and read more frequently than students who do not (Gambrell, 1996). In other words, social collaboration is an important factor in developing confidence and competence as readers.

Kong and Pearson (2003) note that in classrooms with students of diverse cultural and linguistic backgrounds, "comparatively little time is typically spent on comprehension and, especially on meaning construction and authentic communication" (p. 86). Yet, when they studied ELs who read, wrote, and talked about age-appropriate quality literature, they found that those students became more "expert-like and focused" in their conversations over the school year, their command of vocabulary increased dramatically, and they became "more aware of the strategies they were using to construct meaning in response to texts" (p. 86).

Students can use their cognitive strategy bookmarks to annotate their books with Post-it® notes as they read. On several occasions throughout their reading of the text, students compose and share "Lit Letters" (Atwell, 1998) in which they reflect on the texts they are reading (discussing character, plot, setting, theme, etc.), as well as discuss their process, progress, and insights as readers. Students often create artifacts to accompany their letters, such as postcards, found poems, collages, timelines, and so on, often in the voice of a character in the text. The 21st Century Skills English Map (Partnership for 21st Century Skills, 2008) suggests that students write a stylistic imitation of the poem "Where I'm From" by George Ella Lyon (www.georgeellalyon.com) to explore the impact of setting in shaping who they are. In her 12th-grade English language arts class, Barbara Sickler suggested that her students become characters from their chosen books and write and illustrate a Where I'm From poem from their characters' perspectives for their book club. This is an exercise in the cognitive strategy of adopting an alignment. Tierney and Pearson (1983) suggest that having students adopt an alignment by projecting themselves into a text as a character or an eyewitness or object can account for "much of the vibrancy, sense of control, and fulfillment experienced during reading and writing" (p. 573).

Sickler found that this activity was especially beneficial for ELs in her classroom. For example, Jiayuan Liu selected the novel *Winter's Bone* by Daniel Woodrell (2007), adopted an alignment with the main character, Ree Dolly, and wrote and illustrated a Where I'm From poem from his perspective. His poem, in Figure 2.7, and his letter, in Figure 2.8, demonstrate his deep affinity with the character.

Sickler had this to say about Jiayuan's participation in her book club:

> Jiayuan is an avid reader but at times the limitations of his fluency prevented him from expressing exactly what he wanted to say about a text. He found the book club activities very accessible, especially poetry which allowed him more creative freedom to express himself and his reaction to his book. He also enjoyed the visual elements of the book club artifacts. Indeed, several of my EL students said that art allowed them to express their thoughts and feelings when they lacked either the confidence or ability to do so in English. But perhaps the most beneficial aspect of book clubs was the social interaction of meeting to discuss their books. This allowed my EL students to enter into conversation about their books and receive positive feedback and support from a group of peers. Students looked forward to these meetings and

Figure 2.7. Where I'm From Poem

I am from Missouri,

from a cabin and with two kids.

I am from the mystery of losing father.

(With the money he pledged on our house,

And the crazy mother he left over,

With the two little kids,

He disappear)

I am from the cold winter,

the deep forest,

Which blocks away the love

of relatives and friends.

I'm from a single family

and with two younger siblings,

from the father who used to sell drugs and got caught

and my mother who got crazy from that.

From the dad and mom,

From their despicable and useless,

(I got my mom and two kids

I have to raise them and feed them by myself)

From the tragedy which teaches me

And told me to get stronger.

Source: Jiayuan Liu, 2014. Reprinted with permission.

their desire to share their artifacts and literature letters grew as the year progressed. Listening to their book club members talk about their books also increased their motivation to read one of the books they heard discussed.

MODELING WITH MENTOR TEXTS

When Jiayuan Liu wrote his Where I'm From poem in the voice of Ree Dolly in *Winter's Bone*, he used George Ella Lyon's poem as his

Figure 2.8. Student's "Lit Letter"

Dear Book Club,

In *The Winter's Bone*, Ree Dolly is a girl at the age of seventeen that has to rise her family which contain her mother who is mentally ill and her two younger siblings Sonny which is twelve years old brother and Ashlee who is only six. Their family is really poor because of her father Jessup Dolly who was into drug and left the house. She has to not only make sure the family gets food and she also has to take care of her mother. At the mean time, she has to teaches her siblings survival skills not only cooking but hunting too.

One day, Ree found the sheriff around her house who wanted to talk to her mother about her father's case, he bonded on their house and part of their factory, and the police can't find her father anymore. Ree knew that they could lose their house if she can't find her father, so she decided to go on her adventure to find her dad. However, everywhere she went, everyone just pretend to keep silence about her father. It's a world with violence, drug use, even relatives are not nice to her. The story is full of mystery of loosing father and lost in humanities, however, Ree Dolly is strong and brave so I hopes she can find her father and someone nice in the future of the book.

Sincerely,

Jiayuan

Source: Jiayuan Liu, 2014. Reprinted by with permission.

mentor text. Mentor texts are pieces of writing that provide examples of the kind of texts the students are expected to write but may not yet be able to compose by themselves. The teacher can use mentor texts to point out the various features of a given text or genre, thereby enabling students to envision their writing goals. Mentor texts are especially useful in secondary classrooms where there sometimes is a mismatch between the texts students typically read (narrative texts such as stories, poems, etc.) and the texts they are expected to write (informational texts such as essays, reports, etc.) (Pike & Mumper, 2004). For example, students read narratives in their English language arts classrooms and are expected to write analytical essays interpreting them. However, students rarely read essays in class. Providing students with both professional and student models of essays will lessen the textual constraints of writing in an unfamiliar genre. Modeling writing using mentor texts may improve student writing outcomes. A recent meta-analysis of writing instruction in grades 4–12 indicates that guiding students in analyzing mentor texts and emulating "the critical elements, patterns, and forms embodied in the models in their own writing" had positive effects on writing quality (Graham & Perin, 2007, p. 20).

The teacher also can be a source of mentor texts. When teachers write alongside their students in the classroom and model their own composing processes by thinking out loud, students gain insights into the many decisions writers must make as they put pen to paper. They begin to understand that "words do not just magically spill from [their] brain[s] to the paper" but that writing is often difficult, a "struggle" (Gallagher, 2011, p.16). Modeling is especially useful when introducing a new writing task or genre as it can clarify the conventions of the genre and the teacher's expectations, and make visible the skills and strategies necessary to effectively carry out a particular writing task. Modeling thus provides a multi-sensory map that students can access and learn from as they are composing their own texts. It is essential especially for ELs who have limited exposure to texts written in English.

EXPLICIT INSTRUCTION OF ACADEMIC LANGUAGE

Academic language is a key component of effective instruction for ELs (Gersten et al., 2007; Goldenberg, 2013; Rivera et al., 2010; Short & Fitzsimmons, 2007). It is used in school-based text, which structures information efficiently and objectively, involves higher order processes, and integrates multiple linguistic features, including phonology, vocabulary, and discourse. Such text is densely packed with information, objectively written, and dependent on academic content and abstract thinking. It is more decontextualized than conversational language and is characterized by complex sentences and controlled sentence structure, the use of formal grammar, and the application of grammar rules, precision, and tightly organized text. In contrast, informal language is exemplified by the use of slang, everyday words, simple sentence structure, frequent topic shifts, disconnected text, and loose organization (Anstrom et al., 2010; Fillmore & Fillmore, 2012; Snow & Uccelli, 2009).

Teaching academic language explicitly to adolescents figures prominently in the CCSS and is a time-effective way to ensure that ELs gain enough proficiency in academic language to reach rigorous standards. Can't students just acquire it through their interactions with others and their reading? No. English learners often have limited access to proficient speakers of English and even when they do have opportunities to interact with them, ELs are unlikely to hear them using academic language. Moreover, many do not receive much exposure to academic language in their reading, since the reading they do is limited by their language proficiency. They also may avoid reading altogether or skim over texts quickly, reading only for the gist. Fillmore and Fillmore (2012) point out that ELs often encounter challenges in reading academic texts, the very type of writing that could expose them to academic language. Their reading problems can become severe over time, giving rise to increasingly serious challenges that prevent them from acquiring the same features of academic language that their English-speaking classmates acquire subconsciously through their reading. The explicit instruction of academic language can compensate for EL students' inability to develop academic language through their interactions with others and through their reading.

A research-based practice to help EL adolescents catch up so that they can reach grade-level language and writing standards is the explicit instruction of those features of the language that are teachable and are challenging for ELs to acquire on their own, without instruction. Our analysis of language use in thousands of student essays over the past decade reveals that even advanced ELs have difficulties using the following specific, teachable language features, grouped by language category in Figure 2.9 (Olson et al., 2012; Olson & Land, 2007).

The language features in Figure 2.9 are the focus of language standards 1 and 2 (National Governors Association, 2010, pp. 26, 28, 52, 54). They commonly occur across subject areas (social studies, science, mathematics, and English language arts) and are considered part of core academic language (Bailey, 2007). They are strong candidates for explicit instruction since they are teachable and improve students' academic writing.

Below we describe two activities using explicit instruction: one for teaching ELs features of academic language and the other for teaching ELs the ways in which academic language differs from informal language. The activities help ELs reach the following CCR Anchor Standard for Writing CCSS: ELA-Literacy.CCRA.W.4: *Produce clear and coherent writing in which the development and organization are appropriate to task, purpose, and audience.*

Preposition Activity

In the following activity, teachers provide preposition instruction that helps students improve particular writing assignments. Prepositions are especially important for ELs because they have high utility across writing genres (narrative, informational, and

Figure 2.9. Teachable Language Features by Category

Language Category	Sample Sentence Using Feature
Sentence Structure • Avoidance of sentence fragments • Avoidance of run-on sentences	When Martha loved the dog. Jay sat Belinda danced.

Verbs
• Modal auxiliaries
• Verb complements
   o Causative structures
 	
   o Infinitive structures
 	
   o Gerund structures
 	
   o Passive structures
	Concha <u>can</u> drive, but she <u>must</u> not do so at night.
	Enrique **got** Steven **to run** an errand.
	John wants **to go** on a camping trip.
	She avoids **going** to soccer practice.
	Julius Caesar **is murdered by** Brutus.

Markers of Cohesion/Linking Words • Transition words • Word forms	<u>Nevertheless</u>, the people persevered. Although the earthquake devastated the <u>villages</u>, the <u>villagers</u> persevered.
Nouns • Nominalization • Densely packed/modified noun phrases • Plural forms • Subject–verb agreement	The earthquake led to the <u>depletion</u> of valuable resources. The painstaking <u>solidification</u> of the nation The <u>crises</u> increased over the years. The large <u>number</u> of assignments <u>was</u> finally completed.
Articles/determiners/ adjectives	<u>Such</u> earthquakes occurred frequently.

Figure 2.9. Teachable Language Features by Category (continued)

Prepositional Phrases	The book was written <u>by</u> Leonard Pitts.
Vocabulary • Word choice	A <u>patient</u> (instead of <u>this guy</u>) was on a ventilator for many months.
• Fixed expressions (Including Collocations and Idioms)	<u>On the one hand</u>, school uniforms can reduce gang-related crime. <u>On the other hand</u>, they do not necessarily prevent it.
• Adjective + Particle/ preposition combinations	Henry is <u>angry about</u> losing the race.
• Verb + Particle/preposition combinations	The teacher <u>commented on</u> her insightful analysis.

argument writing). Also, as indicated by the example below, they play essential roles in academic writing, allowing writers to pack into their texts dense noun clauses that convey authority and an objective stance, add sentence variety, and introduce critical information about texts, such as authors' names and the titles of texts:

> *In* the Gettysburg Address, a speech delivered *by* Abraham Lincoln *in* 1863, he suggests that the nation was formed *at* the same time as the Declaration *of* Independence, not *at* the time when the Constitution was written.

Prepositions present challenges for ELs. This is because prepositions are used in different ways in different languages, often convey only linguistic relationships rather than content meaning, are unstressed, and occur in thousands of fixed expressions that are used rather infrequently in comparison to content words. Because prepositions lack salience, ELs often do not pay attention to them in the same way that they do content words.

A typical mistake when ELs attempt text-based writing, illustrated by the example below, is to confuse prepositional phrases for the subjects of sentences:

In the Gettysburg Address, by Abraham Lincoln, is about freedom for slaves.

While it is sometimes easiest to teach prepositional phrases as fixed expressions that students memorize as word groups, this approach does not always work. Eventually students will need to learn to create prepositional phrases on their own. Teachers can teach prepositional phrases expediently through explicit instruction. We have found the following instructional steps helpful.

Step 1: Getting the Students Ready and Engaging Their Interest. Here, students learn the lesson objective (learning to use a specific set of prepositions, in this case, *in, on,* and *by*) and revise their own writing to improve their use of prepositions. In setting the stage for learning, teachers might say:

> Today, we will learn to use prepositions and prepositional phrases. When introducing the titles of essays, short stories, and other texts, use prepositional phrases. Using prepositional phrases will make your writing sound academic. They add important details to your writing and increase sentence length and sentence variety.

Step 2: Providing Clear Explanations. Teachers provide student-friendly explanations while their students take notes. The explanations are tied to specific writing tasks, are delivered in the context of writing instruction, build on students' knowledge, and have an immediate effect on improving students' writing. When explaining prepositional phrases, teachers might say:

> Prepositions are words that connect nouns or pronouns to other parts of the sentence. They are like bridges since they link parts of sentences together.

Here is an example of the way teachers can explain how prepositional phrases are used to introduce title, author, and genre (TAG) of a text:

> When writing an introduction to a text-based essay, it is customary to acknowledge the title, the author, and the genre of the work you are discussing. Typically, when you are referring

to the text or the genre, you use the preposition "in," and when you are referring to the author, you use the preposition "by," as in the example below:

TAG: *In* the short story "The Medicine Bag" *by* Native American author Virginia Driving Hawk Sneve, a young boy is confused by his grandfather's heritage.

In the explanation stage, teachers also model how students should use prepositional phrases in writing. They do this by demonstrating the types of thinking the students should use when they are deciding how to use prepositional phrases. They explain the challenges that they themselves face as they use the feature when they are in various stages of the writing process. They remind students that not all small words are prepositions. For example, *an* and *the* are articles, *and* is a conjunction, and *not* is an adverb. They also remind students that prepositional phrases cannot be subjects of sentences. Figure 2.10 provides examples of incorrect and correct uses of prepositional phrases followed by helpful sentence frames for introducing TAGs.

Figure 2.10. Incorrect and Correct Uses of Prepositional Phrases

In the Gettysburg Address, by Abraham Lincoln, is about freedom for slaves.

Prepositional phrase used as subject   *Predicate*

The Gettysburg Address, by Abraham Lincoln, is about freedom for slaves.

Noun phrase used as subject   *Predicate*

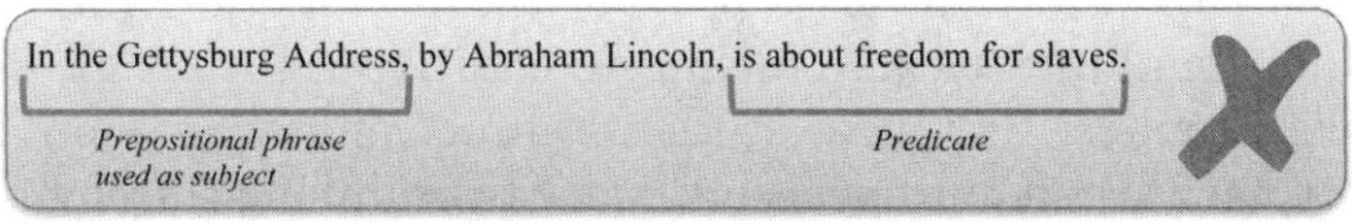

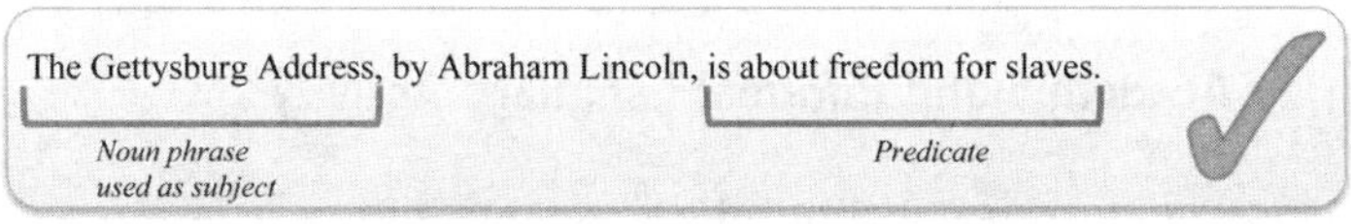

Helpful student frames for tags:

1. *In the narrative* _____ (give the title of the story),

   the author _____ (name the author)

   _____ *claims/states/argues/other reporting verb . . .*

2. *In the narrative* _____ (give the title of the story)

   by _____ (name the author), _____ (name a character) +

   Verb Phrase (tell what the character does, believes, or feels) . . .

Step 3: Providing Practice. Teachers give students additional opportunities to see the language feature used in effective writing and to practice using the feature with others and by themselves. They might ask students to call out the prepositional phrases that are used in the types of TAG statements that they will need to write in their own essays. For example:

> TAG: In the autobiography, *The Long Walk to Freedom*, by Nobel Peace Prize winner and former South African president Nelson Mandela, the author argues that "difficulties break some men but make others."

Teachers also ask students to discuss prepositional phrases in a piece of writing in small groups or with partners and later to add prepositional phrases in a text similar to the one that they are in the process of writing.

Step 4: Providing Formative Assessment. As students practice, teachers monitor and provide feedback on students' use of prepositional phrases in their writing. They glean useful, nuanced information about their students' developing knowledge of prepositions from the students' productive attempts to use them in their writing. They use this information to provide those students who need it with additional instruction, including additional text analyses and practice. Further, they give students direct encouragement to attempt to use targeted prepositions prior to or during the completion of the writing assignment.

Comparing Academic and Informal Language Activity

In a different activity designed to teach academic language, students learn to distinguish between informal and academic language and to make their own writing more academic. Learning to recognize the differences between academic and informal language is essential to knowing when to use the features of one register and when to use the features of the other. Identifying differences in register builds students' metalinguistic awareness, enabling students to reflect on language, manipulate it to convey meaning, and maintain consistency in register use, thereby boosting their writing ability (Schleppegrell, 2013).

In the activity, teachers begin by helping students identify the features of academic writing in a given text. After explicitly discussing the general characteristics of academic and informal writing, teachers create two essays, one written in informal English and another written in academic English, seaming together portions of essays that their students previously composed. They make sure to include, in the informal essays, the types of linguistic features that they want students to avoid in academic writing. In analyzing student writing, we have found that these features include general words like *nice, story,* or *man* instead of more academic or technical ones like *compassionate, narrative,* or *novelist*; slang like *stuff, guy,* and *blown away*; inappropriate hedges like *kind of* and *sort of*; informal expressions and markers of spoken English like *ya know* and *by the way*; needless repetition; misspellings; grammatical errors; contractions; poorly linked sentences with an absence of clear referents; the unnecessary or redundant use of I (e.g., *I think . . .* followed by plot summary or *In my opinion, I believe that . . .*); and simple rather than complex sentences with little sentence variety.

After discussing the linguistic features in the two essays with others, students can work in pairs to revise a sample informal paragraph (see Figure 2.11).

SCAFFOLDING INSTRUCTION FOR ENGLISH LEARNERS

Scaffolding breaks learning into chunks and then provides tools to help students understand each chunk, so that teachers can provide academically challenging instruction to those who need additional conceptual, academic, and linguistic support. It can help ELs flourish as writers (Juel, 1994), giving them multiple forms of high-level assistance. The concept of scaffolding is based on the work of Lev Vygotsky (1934/1986), who proposed that with adult assistance, children accomplish tasks that they ordinarily cannot perform independently. In extending his colleague's work, Jerome Bruner (1983) used the term *scaffold* in reference to the "process of 'setting

Figure 2.11. Essay Introduction in Informal English

<u>Well</u>, <u>this</u> <u>story</u> by <u>Leonard</u> is about Haiti. <u>Alot</u> of people over there <u>gotta</u> accept the earth is cruel and they <u>gotta</u> suffer <u>cuz</u> of a big earthquake. It is not <u>there</u> fault. <u>In my opinion, I think</u> Haitians could not <u>of</u> stopped the shaking cuz they did not make <u>the shaking</u>. <u>But</u> the men and women over there gotta be <u>pretty</u> brave. <u>And</u> they need to learn to <u>live</u> even if there is a lot of rain. <u>What's up with that?</u>

Note that in this paragraph, the informal words in need of revision are underlined.

up' the situation to make the child's entry easy and successful and then gradually pulling back and handing the role to the child as he becomes skilled enough to manage it" (p. 60). In Bruner's view, adults can give children support until they are able to apply new skills and strategies independently.

Students need to develop their competence to read and write texts not only with their teachers' guidance and with the support of their classmates, but also on their own. They will read and write many types of texts by themselves at school, in their communities, and at their work. This means that their teachers must take time to plan activities that shift the responsibility of learning, reading, and writing to the students, so that the students are able to complete reading and writing assignments independently. In describing this process, Pearson and Gallagher (1983) coined the term "gradual release of responsibility." In their model, students move from explicit instruction and modeling to guided, collaborative practice with partners and groups, and finally to independent practice. Four parts of a lesson that shifts responsibility to learners, presented by Fisher and Frey (2011), are:

1. The Focus Lesson: "I Do It." (The teacher completes a task in front of the students; this involves teacher explanation, modeling, and/or demonstration.)
2. Guided Instruction: "We Do It." (The teacher guides the students, step by step, taking the lesson apart in manageable chunks; the students, with the teacher's guidance, complete reading and writing assignments.)
3. Collaborative Instruction: "You Do It Together." (The students complete a task with classmates, for instance, during pair and group activities.)
4. Independent: "You Do It Alone." (The students work on their own to complete a task.)

The activities described earlier in this chapter that teach academic language features (prepositions) and the differences between academic and informal writing illustrate ways teachers can shift responsibility for learning to students, empowering them to become competent readers and writers.

Many scaffolding theories and models have been developed (Gibbons, 2002; Rogoff, 1990; Tharp & Gallimore, 1991). All involve teachers providing specific scaffolds. These include graphic organizers; word banks; sentence, paragraph, and essay models and templates; and outlines. They foster students' development of a wide variety of cognitive and language competencies, helping them construct just the right sentences and discourse structures required to explain, describe, or clarify what they want to communicate. Using language scaffolds lessens students' affective, linguistic, and cognitive loads, helping students get their words together, giving them language, and preventing them from losing their focus. This in turn allows them to concentrate on their ideas and convey them in writing. Let's look at two scaffolding activities that have been highlighted by Goldenberg (2013) as being especially beneficial for ELs.

Graphic Organizer Activity

Graphic organizers include T-charts, concept maps, webs, mind maps, note-taking templates, and more. T-charts, such as that in Figure 2.12, help students develop their ability to describe similarities and differences, for example, between themes, events, characters, and settings in literary texts, and between evidence, important concepts, and events in persuasive writing and informational texts. Graphic organizers visually display critical relationships between concepts, facts, and ideas. In so doing, they enable students to "step back, analyze text closely, form preliminary interpretations, and seek validation for interpretations" (Olson, 2011, p. 138). They are particularly helpful in developing ideas for writing. In Figure 2.12 an 8th-grader uses a T-chart to compare and contrast two characters, Roger and Mrs. Louella Bates Washington Jones, described in Langston Hughes' (1998) short story, "Thank You, Ma'am."

To help ELs gain the English proficiency to complete the assignment, the teacher can begin the assignment with the entire class, brainstorming and giving examples of appropriate similarities and differences, and ask students to work with pairs with word banks or sentence strips before completing the assignment on their own.

Sentence Frames Activity

To help ELs organize their writing, teachers also can give students a different type of scaffolding template that students can refer to as they write. Sentence frames are especially helpful in accelerating learners' development of the complex sentence structures needed in writing (Zwiers, 2008). English learners who have difficulty producing comparative structures can benefit from sentence frames such as those in Figure 2.13.

Figure 2.12. T-Chart Comparison of Roger and Mrs. Louella Bates Washington Jones

Similarities	Differences
Both are African Americans.	One is male and the other is female.
Both are outside of the place they live on the same evening.	One is caring and the other is self-centered.
Both want to gain the other's confidence.	One injures (by stealing) and the other is the injured.
Both regret some past actions.	One is a kid and the other an adult.
Both probably want a sense of security.	One is mature and the other is immature.

FORMATIVE ASSESSMENT

Among the 15 elements of effective adolescent literacy programs, Biancarosa and Snow (2004) have theorized that three are most critical to improving student outcomes: (1) ongoing and sustained professional development to improve teacher practice; (2) the use of summative outcomes to evaluate efficacy; and (3) the use of formative assessment to inform instructional activities. Frequent formative assessment is especially important for improving the academic literacy of ELs. It enables teachers to gauge the effectiveness of their writing instruction and shape their instructional practices to their students' needs. It also provides students with essential information about their writing strengths and weaknesses, and delivers it in a nonthreatening, objective way. This type of assessment includes writing rubrics; informative feedback, for example, with editing marks and comments in the margins of students' papers; checklists; self-evaluations and reflections; peer reviews; teacher conferences; and ongoing portfolio reviews (Graham, Harris, & Hebert, 2011). Fisher and Frey (2011) present a variety of practical assessments to correct students' misconceptions and improve their knowledge of academic language features.

In Chapter 1, we described Marisela Gonzalez's analysis of the theme in "Sometimes, the Earth Is Cruel." Fortunately, Marisela's teacher used her writing to assess her strengths and weaknesses and help her improve her writing. The teacher encouraged Marisela, drawing attention to her many strengths, such as her efforts to use academic words (*memorialize*) and complex sentences to convey authority, her use of quotation, her developing ability to use transition words such as *also* to link sentences, and her

Figure 2.13. Sentence Frames for Compare and Contrast

Describing Similarities

The traits they have in common are _____.

They are similar because _____.

Both are the same because _____.

Their shared/common attributes are _____.

They are similar in that _____.

The way they are alike is that they both are/have _____.

By comparison, _____ is _____.

In comparison, _____ is _____.

Describing Differences

The differences between _____ and _____ are _____.

A distinction between _____ and _____ might be _____.

_____ is _____-er than _____.

_____ is _____-er than _____, but _____-er than _____.

_____ is _____-er than _____.

_____ and _____ are similar because they both are/have _____.

They are different because _____ is _____ and _____ is _____.

A notable difference (key distinction) between _____ and _____ is _____.

Other Expressions to Show Differences and Similarities

Neither _____ nor_____ has/contains/demonstrates/shows _____.

_____ is/tends to be _____, whereas _____ is/tends to be _____.

ability to engage the reader's attention by using vivid examples. The teacher also gave her a short list of language features to work on improving. They included spelling (*exept, sufferd, lttel, Gought, reboit, earthquak, bing, meony*), sentence structure (*so people can see what will happen if that was us; That what people did to help people that were very sick. Thats why we should be happy to be safe*), converting informal English (like *stuff*) to more academic English, and modal auxiliaries like *would* (*when it raind it will not stop for days*).

OPPORTUNITIES TO PRACTICE

In the Institute of Education Sciences (IES) Practice Guide *Teaching Elementary Students to Be Effective Writers* (Graham et al., 2012), the first recommendation is *Provide daily time for students to write.* This might seem so obvious that it wouldn't need to be mentioned; however, recent surveys of elementary teachers indicate that students spend little time writing during the school day (Cutler & Graham, 2008; Gilbert & Graham, 2010). A national survey of high school teachers' reported writing practices indicates that secondary students also lack opportunities to write as a routine component of their classroom instruction (Kiuhara, Graham, & Hawken, 2009). In fact, almost one half of the participating teachers did not assign at least one multi-paragraph writing assignment monthly. Another national study of writing conducted by Applebee and Langer (2011) confirms that much of the writing students do in secondary school is short (less than a paragraph) and does not provide students with the opportunities "to use composing as a way to think through the issues, to show the depth and breadth of their knowledge, or to go beyond what they know in making connections or raising new issues" (p. 16). Perhaps this is why the National Commission on Writing (2003) recommends that schools double the amount of time students spend writing in school.

It is ironic that struggling writers and ELs, students who might benefit most from writing practice, often spend the least amount of time engaged in authentic, extended writing activities. One might hope that Gallagher's (2006) description of the EL classroom, quoted below, might be an anomaly, but many other researchers (Gándara, Rumberger, Maxwell-Jolly, & Callahan, 2003) have corroborated his observation:

Recently I visited a classroom in which ELLs spent forty-five minutes diagramming sentences. There was no hint of authentic reading or writing. There was no evidence of genuine fluency building. There was also no classroom library. This is not an isolated incident—I have seen similar evidence of low expectations in other ELL classrooms as well. (p. 10)

He adds, "Though a cliché, the old adage is true: no one rises to low expectations" (p. 10).

The expert IES panel (Graham et al., 2012) recommends that teachers devote at least 1 hour per day to writing. However, noting that practice alone is insufficient to guarantee writing improvement, the panel suggests that at least 30 minutes of that hour be allocated to teaching a variety of writing strategies, techniques, and skills appropriate to students' levels of proficiency. Especially critical for ELs is providing instruction in how to write complex texts and ongoing opportunities to practice writing in specific genres on diverse topics for a variety of audiences and purposes. In particular, ELs need time and practice in exploring textual references, gathering and organizing information, analyzing evidence, and defending their ideas in order to produce the type of well-reasoned arguments in extended pieces of essay writing emphasized in the Common Core State Standards.

To Sum Up

- Research tells us that ELs benefit from clear instructions and supportive guidance; effective modeling of skills, strategies, and procedures; active student engagement and participation; effective feedback; practice and periodic review; and regular assessments.

- ELs need culturally relevant writing instruction that capitalizes on the funds of knowledge they bring to the learning task. Practices that facilitate connections between students and their classrooms, homes, and communities tap into the strengths that ELs bring with them to school.

- Strategy instruction has been widely accepted as one of the most effective practices for literacy development, not only for ELs but for all students. It helps students to understand, interpret, and write essays about complex texts by providing them with an explicit focus on language, by increasing their exposure to academic texts, by making the texts they read comprehensible, and by providing them with the means of learning language on their own, outside of class.

- Modeling appropriate language use and processes of connecting reading and writing is also important as is scaffolding instruction using graphic organizers, mentor texts, and other meaningful visuals to support student learning.
- ELs need explicit instruction in academic English, opportunities to practice and develop this complex register of language, and formative assessment to monitor progress and craft ongoing instruction.

CHAPTER 3

Narrative Writing and CCSS

Recognizing the importance of narrative writing at the secondary level for all learners, the authors of the CCR Anchor Standards for Writing developed the following standard: Write narratives to develop real or imagined experiences or events using effective technique, well-chosen details, and well-structured event sequences. Narrative writing conveys "experience, either real or imaginary, and uses time as its deep structure. It can be used for many purposes, such as to inform, instruct, persuade, or entertain" and includes creative fictional stories, memoirs, anecdotes, and autobiographies (National Governors Association, Appendix A, p. 26). Furthermore, it increases students' ability to write "visual details of scenes, objects, or people; to depict specific actions (e.g., movements, gestures, postures, and expressions); to use dialogue and interior monologue that provide insight into the narrator's and characters' personalities and motives; and to manipulate pace to highlight the significance of events and create tension and suspense" (CCSS, Appendix A, p. 23).

In addition to explaining the skills and knowledge pertinent to narrative writing that students are to master (CCSS, Appendix C), the CCSS clarify the ways teachers are to prioritize their instruction of narratives. Table 3.1 outlines the percentage of instructional time that teachers should devote to the teaching of narrative, informational, and argumentative writing in the upper grades.

Table 3.1. Distribution of Communicative Purposes by Grade in the 2011 NAEP Writing Framework

Grade Level	Narrative	Informational	Argumentative
4	35%	35%	30%
8	30%	35%	35%
12	20%	40%	40%

Source: National Assessment Governing Board (2007). Writing framework for the 2011 National Assessment of Educational Progress, pre-publication edition. Iowa City, IA: ACT, Inc. (CCSS p. 5).

Often overlooked is the very important footnote that the percentages reported in the table reflect the sum of students' reading and writing across all disciplines, not just in ELA settings. As the table and footnote indicate, the CCSS mandate that teachers spend significant instructional time teaching narrative writing, which decreases in the upper grades, as students acquire the ability to produce narratives.

A key departure from earlier standards is the emphasis in the CCSS on the complex nature of narrative writing. In the CCSS documents, narrative writing becomes more formal and academic in the upper grades. Its language demands call on students "to communicate clearly to an external, sometimes unfamiliar audience" (Appendix A, p. 26), to produce numerous narratives "over short and extended time frames throughout the year" (Appendix A, p. 26), and to use complex language and rhetorical forms to convey meaning precisely and effectively.

WHY PRIORITIZE NARRATIVE WRITING WITH ENGLISH LEARNERS?

Narrative writing plays a critical role in the CCSS and has tremendous potential in helping ELs develop their English and succeed in ELA coursework in the secondary grades. At a particularly difficult time in their lives, when they might worry that their limited resources in English could conceal their cognitive abilities and capability of expressing themselves, narrative writing enables ELs to make use of their community knowledge and previous linguistic resources, including their knowledge of informal oral English, their first languages, and diverse varieties of English. It builds directly on what they know. It even allows them to evaluate their experiences in the United States, leading to the development of their personal identities and identities as writers (Meltzer & Hamann, 2005; Short & Fitzsimmons, 2007). Beyond this, it provides teachers with ways to inventory what ELs know about language and writing, build on student knowledge, and familiarize themselves with their students' cultures, communities, and experiences.

Although the CCSS present narrative text after informational/ expository and argumentative texts, we have reversed this order for these reasons: (1) to build on ELs' existing knowledge of genres and text structures, previous knowledge, and linguistic resources; (2) to motivate them; (3) to provide a strong basis for their development of other types of writing; and (4) to contribute to their reading development and understanding of literature.

All students have ideas for stories that they have gained through their life experiences and are able to utilize their previous knowledge to develop narratives. As a number of researchers have pointed out, by the time children enter kindergarten, most students in the United States are familiar with narrative texts and are able to link real events to stories they have heard (see, e.g., Heath's 1986 seminal article). Like monolingual English speakers, ELs often are highly familiar with narratives, since this text type often is presented to them through oral and written stories in their homes, schools, and communities (Schleppegrell, 2009). Narratives represent shared understandings of human experience and, as such, are a culture's "coin and currency" (Bruner, 2003, p. 15), essential in communicating real-life experiences. Children engage in language play and fantasy talk, and they learn to interact with others, for example, jointly discussing toys, pictures, and activities. By the time they reach adolescence, they have gained a variety of narrative skills, which they have learned naturally in everyday communicative environments. Through their discussions, they have learned what appropriate topics are, how to stay on topic, how to give enough information to their audiences, and how to communicate acceptably, expressing themselves coherently (Snow & Beals, 2006).

Many other researchers also have emphasized the pivotal role of narratives in motivating students and building their confidence as writers. Hillocks (2007), for instance, argues that narrative writing is inherently interesting to learners since it allows them to write about meaningful experiences, reflect on them, bring these experiences into perspective, and learn from them. Teenagers, especially, use narratives to explore their own identities, the way they see themselves. Consequently, they are generally highly motivated to write about the stories of their own lives and the lives of others. Like Hillocks, expert education researcher Ann Mechem Ziergiebel (2013) argues, "Whether stories are read or written in school or out of school, students become engaged and motivated by just a turn of a phrase, a voice, an image, or a character, conflict, setting, or theme" (p. 140).

Narrative writing not only motivates students to write; it is the key to their progress in learning other types of writing, such as persuasive and report writing (see, e.g., Fredricksen, Wilhelm, & Smith, 2012). It helps students develop audience awareness, organizational skills, and the ability to select and use specific, concrete details, all of which are key in informational and argumentative writing. Narrative writing also helps students develop vocabulary, morphology, and sentence structure, leading to improved sentence variety. It elicits a wide variety of linguistic features, including a full range of cohesive devices; complex noun phrases and descriptive clauses, phrases, and words; and verb tenses (Labov & Waletzky, 1967). These language features form a foundation for the development of other types of linguistic skills (Uccelli, Hemphill, Pan, & Snow, 2005). Ultimately, narrative writing contributes to students' ability to read literature critically. As Hillocks (2007) points out, it allows them to "understand more fully how the works of professional writers are constructed" (p. 1) and identify from their reading the particular techniques that will be useful in their own writing.

All students, and particularly ELs, have much more difficulty learning to write informational and argumentative texts when they have not first learned to write narrative texts. They have, in the past, had limited exposure to informational and argumentative texts and limited opportunities to discuss and compose them. Also, they often do not identify with the topics of informational and argumentative texts and lack the personal experiences and background knowledge to relate to these topics to the same extent as they identify with the topics of narrative writing. Hence, we discuss informational and argumentative writing last, given the challenges these two types of texts present to both teachers and students.

THE LANGUAGE DEMANDS OF NARRATIVE WRITING

Narration, the telling of factual and imaginary stories, creates a clear picture in the readers' minds of something that happens, with a setting, characterization, and plot. Short stories, personal essays and letters, diary entries, biographical works, and travelogues all contain narrative writing. Their basic purpose is to entertain, although they also may be written to teach, inform, or even change attitudes. When organizing narratives, writers generally include a title, as well as an introduction, in which the characters, setting, and time of the story are established; a body, in which the complication involving the main characters is conveyed; and a concluding section, in which the resolution of the complication is communicated.

Writers often begin their narratives with short, timeless phrases (*Long ago in a far-off land*), generic settings, and generic characters. They generally convey the events using either a chronological ordering or a series of flashbacks. Following the principle of "showing, not telling," they evoke the five senses, provide dialogue, and describe events using multiple vivid examples to reveal theme, plot, resolution, and characterization. They use a variety of sentence structures and may use hyperbole or deliberate exaggeration to make their writing dramatic or humorous. Although there are variations, most writers begin narratives with the present tense and switch to the past tense when describing the elements of stories and then back to the present tense when writing their conclusions. They generally avoid the passive voice, using action verbs like *scream*, *bounce*, and *speed* to show what is happening. The vocabulary varies greatly, but often includes emphatic words (*certainly*, *truly*, *definitely*) that convey certainty; onomatopoeic words, like *buzz*, with sounds imitating their meaning; and specific words (like *orchid*) instead of general words (like *flower*).

CHALLENGES OF NARRATIVE WRITING FOR ENGLISH LEARNERS

Many ELs and others have difficulty learning to write the types of formal, academic narratives required by the CCSS. They often acquire the ability to tell informal stories orally, and these types of stories give no indication of the relative timing of events. In contrast to these informal stories, academic ones provide adverbial time markers like *first, then,* or *next,* as well as adverbial time clauses that create complex relationships between events and indicate when events take place. Students' informal narratives may contain unclear references, include irrelevant information, lack a central idea that unifies the text, and omit key components, such as the introduction or evaluative elements. They may lack the formal organization of narratives required in academic writing, and they may include vernacular forms of English grammar and learner English such as the use of adjacent words instead of possessive adjectives (like *John house* instead of *John's house*). Learners may produce informal narratives largely because they have not yet been taught how to write academic ones and because they tend to use the language resources with which they are most familiar. Rather than penalize students for their lack of knowledge of the required features of academic narratives, it is a good idea to teach them these features and ways to incorporate informal language into the rich dialogues contained in their narratives.

Learning to incorporate dialogue is enormously challenging for ELs who may have entered U.S. schools at a grade level where it is assumed that they already know how to punctuate dialogue and incorporate it into their writing as a device to support ideas and add key information about stance, beliefs, facial expressions, and actions. Learning to use indirect quotations (such as *John told him to run*) is one of the most difficult linguistic skills ELs need to learn, because in order to produce these indirect quotations they must be able to construct complex sentences with verb complements (like *to run*). These problems are confounded since ELs are still learning to adhere to English subject–verb agreement and verb tense consistency rules. Many ELs who have lived in the United States for many years delete third person -s forms, since this form does not exist in the dialect of English they have learned (Labov, 1972). Many also do not use verb tense endings such as the -ed ending on "talked." Hence, when introducing quotations, they might write, "Today John yell come here," deleting verb endings after *yell* and the required punctuation marks.

Particular challenges for ELs at the intermediate levels of English learning include understanding and following the principle of showing, not telling; using a variety of sentence structures, especially those with participles, prepositional phrases, and gerunds; switching between verb tenses; establishing cohesion (e.g., through transition words and other more subtle linguistic features like sentence complexity and pronouns); incorporating noun modifiers (especially phrases and clauses) to convey precise details; maintaining pronoun consistency; and using vivid and specific vocabulary, and fixed expressions (including phrases like all of *a* sudden, not all of *the* sudden, or, on the *other hand*, not on the *another hands*).

English learners at the beginning levels of English proficiency have all the above challenges but also have many problems forming sentences and using basic vocabulary. Without adequate word knowledge, students are challenged to narrate experiences. For example, to be meaningful, most narratives must include evaluative statements, and these statements require considerable vocabulary knowledge. Actions make most sense when writers know the actors' motivation and intentions, and stories are more engaging when they relate the actors' emotions and desires and the narrator's reactions. Beginning-level ELs' narratives tend to discuss simple emotions or desires of the characters—happiness, sadness, fear, and anger in the case of emotion, and what they want or like in the case of desires. Their restricted vocabulary prevents them from providing more effective evaluations. This can be frustrating to ELs, who are in no way cognitively deficient and whose developing knowledge of English prevents them from showing what they know and expressing critical meaning. Their instructors need to help them express more complex emotions like surprise, guilt, or jealousy and to refer to the characters' cognitive states (e.g., what they believe, know, or are thinking about). Beginning-level learners have limited fluency and accuracy, and require much scaffolding (e.g., narrative templates, sentence stems, word and sentence banks, pictorial supports, and graphic organizers).

TEACHING THE ELEMENTS OF NARRATIVE WRITING

Whether students write narratives to develop real or imagined events, they will need to develop a plot or story line, organize an event sequence, introduce a narrator and/or characters, create a setting, use narrative techniques and relevant descriptive details to capture the action and convey experiences and events, and provide a conclusion that resolves, follows from, or reflects upon the narrated experiences or events. Those are the basics. Emma Coats (n.d.), former employee at Pixar, an animation film studio currently owned by the Walt Disney Studio and producer of films such as *Toy Story* and *Finding Nemo*, tweeted 22 handy rules of storytelling that teachers can access in a slideshow format to help students make the most out of their stories. Here are some of our favorites:

1. Why must you tell THIS story? What's the belief burning within you that your story feeds off of? That's the heart of it.
2. If you were a character in this situation, how would you feel? Honesty lends credibility to unbelievable situations.
3. What are the stakes? Give us a reason to root for the character. What happens if they don't succeed?
4. Putting it on paper lets you start fixing it. If it stays in your head, a perfect idea, you'll never share it with anyone.

After students write their narratives, they can vote on which of Pixar's rules they found most helpful. ELs have rich and heartfelt stories to tell, but they will need assistance with developing the elements of narrative writing. The following strategies and activities can make the task of narrative writing more accessible.

Story Mountain Activity

Every story must have a beginning. The start or *exposition* is where the characters and setting are established. During this part of a story, a *conflict* usually is introduced. After the characters and the main circumstances are introduced, a problem often arises that puts the character in crisis. This is the *rising action* of the story. It typically is followed by a *climax* or high point that involves a major challenge or dark moment the characters must overcome. This often includes a turning point in the story. Following the climax, the story begins to wind down. During the *falling action*, we see the results of the characters' actions or decisions. This leads to the *resolution* or denouement ("unraveling") where the story concludes, often conveying a lesson or theme.

One way to make these plot elements more comprehensible to ELs is to introduce the concept of a story mountain, a user-friendly simplification of Aristotle's W-diagram. Figure 3.1 introduces the Story Mountain formula.

Since the best way to learn how to write narratives is to read them, students can read a number of narratives and work in groups to fill out the Story Mountain before using the graphic organizer to sequence their own narratives.

Older students and more proficient students can experiment with the Plot Poem, an example of which is shown in Figure 3.2 about the novel *The Kite Runner* (Hosseini, 2003).

Challenges that ELs might face when participating in the Story Mountain activity include describing results of the characters'

Figure 3.1. Story Mountain

actions and decisions with causative verbs such as *cause, allow, influence, force,* and *make,* which are used to indicate that someone or something helps to make something happen. As indicated by the following sentences, causative verbs are used in different grammatical patterns that are similar enough to confuse students: John *enabled* him *to tell* the truth; She *forced* him *into confessing*; and Paul *made* his brothers clean the kitchen. Students also may find it challenging to learn transition words such as *hence, consequently, therefore,* and *as a result,* especially when these words are used as sentence interrupters that are set off by commas: Mabel's decision to give her friend some lunch money, *therefore,* demonstrated her kindness.

Faces Vocabulary and the Character Evolution Timeline Activities

"Characters are the heart and soul of every story" (Donovan, n.d.). They are an essential element in making a story compelling. When Katniss Everdeen volunteers to take her sister's place as a tribute in *The Hunger Games* by Suzanne Collins (2008), we are struck by her bravery and resolve. And when she is lifted into the arena and beholds the Cornucopia at the start of the games, we feel her

Figure 3.2. Plot Poem

1. *Exposition:* With a phone call Rahim Khan gives the story a push
2. *Setting:* back into the tumult in the shadow of the Hindu Kush.
3. *Protagonist:* American Amir, the princely writer, with a guilty heart
4. *Inciting in:* must go and make amends or be forever torn apart.
5. *Antagonist:* Class warfare, religion, and politics battle for his soul.
6. *Conflict:* He must face the truth head-on to again be whole.
7. *Rising:* Baba is dying of brain cancer, the wedding cannot wait.
8. *Action:* Soraya cannot produce children. Oh what a cruel fate.
9. *Crisis:* "Hassan is my brother!" That pain was only fleeting.
10. *Climax:* Amir stands up for Hassan and takes a brutal beating.
11. *Falling Action:* He cuts through the red tape and saves Hassan's heir.
12. *Resolution:* Sohrab now has a father and mother who will care.
13. *Theme:* A man can stand up for himself at any time.
14. *Theme (2):* It is never too late to be good again, no matter what the crime.

Source: Sachin Parekh 2014. Reprinted with permission.

trepidation and root for her as she runs for cover, convinced that her strength of character will enable her to overcome challenges and to prevail. As mentioned previously, English learners may be frustrated by their limited ability to depict personality traits or express complex emotions that would give their characters more depth. One way to help them move beyond *happy, sad, mad,* and *glad,* popularized by English teacher Nelma Anselmi is to present them with the Faces Vocabulary Chart (www.pinterest.com/pin/459015386993518541/). This chart includes 41 facial expressions in alphabetical order from *aggressive* to *withdrawn.* These faces can be explicitly taught in relation to literature students are reading and can be cut up and put into envelopes for students to sort (negative to positive, synonyms/antonyms, degrees of an emotion, i.e., *happy* to *ecstatic,* etc.). A chart of facial expressions with the adjectives removed also can be given to ELs along with a word bank. Students then select which adjective from the word bank best describes each expression, thus enhancing their repertoire of emotion words.

To help ELs develop their vocabulary expediently, teachers are wise to first teach them high-utility sensory words that the students can use frequently in their narratives and other genres, words that they do not already know, as well as words with big word families. To prevent students from confusing words, it is probably a good idea to present just a reasonable number of words to students and to teach them word sets that are not similar in appearance or do not overlap in meaning, for example, *arrogant, miserable, lonely, frustrated,* and so on. Once students have expanded their vocabulary, they can develop a Character Evolution Timeline.

A Character Evolution Timeline enables a reader to review the sequence of events that occur in a text and to plot it out graphically, much like one would with a storyboard. However, in the graphic display, the reader can chart a character's changing emotions by selecting: (1) a facial expression to reveal the character's emotions during key events; (2) a quote that illustrates why or how the character experiences this emotion; and (3) a symbol to characterize that emotion. Beneath the quote, the reader can write an interpretation of the impact of the event on the character in his or her own words. This is a great exercise in character analysis, analyzing an author's craft, and forming interpretations. Figure 3.3 includes a Character Evolution Timeline for the character of Rachel in "Eleven" by Sandra Cisneros (2002) and illustrates the range of emotions she experiences on her 11th birthday when her teacher, Mrs. Price, forces her to wear an ugly red sweater that isn't hers.

Figure 3.3. Character Evolution Timeline

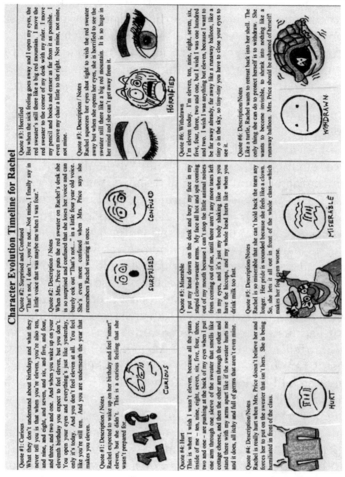

Once students, as readers, have traced a character's emotional evolution in a model text, they can use the timeline strategy to plot out their own story lines as writers and to record emotions in relation to event sequences and even to record ideas for dialogue and interior monologue.

Character Evolution Timelines provide teachers with excellent opportunities to teach students parallel structure, challenges for all students, but especially for ELs. Writers use parallel structures, the same pattern of words, to indicate that two or more ideas are more or less equivalent in importance. Generally, when writing Character Evolution Timelines, the event sequences are written consistently in one tense, the present tense or past tense, as in: *Like a turtle, Rachel wants to retreat into her shell. The only thing she can do to protect herself is to withdraw.* Other challenges learners encounter in the Character Evolution Timelines include subject–verb agreement issues (especially if the student chooses to use the present tense) and concerns pertaining to using appropriate word forms (more specifically, expressing a range of emotions with words of the correct part of speech—*surprisingly, surprise,* or *surprising*).

Said Is Dead Activity

In the same way that ELs may be limited by their ability to express a range of emotions, they also may have difficulty writing dialogue between characters that flows and departs from a typical "he said; she said" structure. It is not appropriate to "kill" off the word *said* until ELs are familiar with the conventions of writing dialogue, have practiced reading dialogues in mentor texts, have orally read dialogues in pairs to familiarize themselves with the turn-taking involved, and have attempted writing simple dialogue exchanges. But when the teacher determines students are ready, she can introduce the tombstone in Figure 3.4 and post it on the wall.

Beneath the area that says "survived by," students can add words to use instead of said, for example, *cried, fussed, grunted, moaned, mumbled, roared, shrieked, wailed,* and so on. Students can consult the tombstone as they develop their narratives, write dialogue, and add dialogue tags. Teachers will want to teach or review the meanings of these words, as it is likely that ELs will not know them. They will find it helpful to give ELs repeated opportunities to match the meanings of the words with emotions, and to show students how to use the words that are appropriate alternatives to "said" to express emotions (like *excitement, anger, agitation, sadness, happiness*). They also will find it effective to teach words that can occur next to the alternative words, for example, "My brother *mournfully* wailed, 'Oh no!' as his favorite toy fell from the window onto the street below" or "Erick shrieked *in horror*, 'Fire!'"

Punctuating dialogue is particularly challenging for ELs, and teachers will want to take the opportunity to teach (or reteach) students effective ways of incorporating dialogue. Another challenge ELs may face is how to incorporate words from informal English (and possibly even words from their home languages that are translated) into their dialogues when writing for an unfamiliar audience. Teachers will want to demonstrate ways to do this. For example, teachers might present the following unpunctuated excerpt from "Eleven" and ask students to work in pairs to punctuate the

Figure 3.4. Said Is Dead

dialogue. The teacher might say, "Rewrite the paragraphs I give you including the correct punctuation—capital letters, periods, commas, question marks, and quotation marks. I have included the correct punctuation in the opening quotation for you as a model":

> "Whose is this?" Mrs. Price says, as she holds the red sweater up in the air for all the class to see it's been sitting in the classroom for a month not mine says everybody not me.

Vocabulary of the Senses, Word Wall and Showing, Not Telling Activities

Sensory/descriptive writing is based on concrete details. Writers gather information through all five senses and use those details to present a word picture of a person, place, object, or event. The goal is to choose precise words to enable the reader to visualize what is being described. One way to begin developing sensory descriptive language is to create a Vocabulary of the Senses Word Wall in the classroom, as shown in Figure 3.5.

The teacher might begin with a sensory experience, such as popping popcorn, where students can see the hard kernels transformed into fluffy white puffs, hear the sizzling of the oil and the tiny explosions of kernels popping, smell the aroma of melted butter, and feel the crunchiness of each morsel as they happily munch on the delicious snack. As the students read narratives in class, they can add "juicy" descriptive words to the word wall. When they compose narratives, they can select vocabulary words from the different sense categories to make their writing more precise. Beginning writers tend to rely most heavily on the sense of sight, so the teacher should encourage them to include the other senses in their writing as well.

Once students are familiar with sensory descriptive language, the teacher can introduce the concept of showing, not telling. She might begin by saying the following:

> When writers show and don't just tell in their writing, they use rich, descriptive language to dramatize what is happening and provide concrete details that paint pictures in readers' minds. Here are two examples, one of telling writing and one of showing writing:
>
> *Context:* In Gary Soto's (1990) story, "Seventh Grade," Victor enrolls in French class because he wants to impress Teresa, the girl he has a crush on. When Mr. Bueller, the teacher, asks if anyone in class knows how to speak French, Victor raises his hand, even though he doesn't really know how to speak the language. So, Mr. Bueller says something to Victor in French. Now, Victor is really in a tight spot.
>
> Gary Soto could have just told us how Victor felt. He might have written a few telling sentences such as the following:
>
> *Telling:* Victor was really embarrassed. He knew he was going to look stupid. But he was stuck. So, he uttered a few pretend words in French.
>
> Here's the showing description that Soto actually wrote:
>
> *Showing:* "Great rose bushes of red bloomed on Victor's cheeks. A river of nervous sweat ran down his palms. He felt awful. Teresa sat a few desks away, no doubt thinking he was a

Figure 3.5. Vocabulary of the Senses Word Wall

See	Hear	Smell	Taste	Touch
Darkened	Bawl	Fragrant	Appetizing	Coarse
Gloomy	Groan	Fresh	Spicy	Greasy
Sparkling	Mumble	Pungent	Stale	Scratchy
Transparent	Screech	Stuffy	Yummy	Slimy

fool. Without looking at Mr. Bueller, Victor mumbled, 'Frenchie oh wewe gee in September.'"

This shows us that Victor was embarrassed without directly telling us. It is much easier to picture in our minds how he looked and felt when Mr. Bueller put him on the spot.

After providing this example, the teacher might ask students what words or expressions they could use to dramatize the word *nervous* in the sentence *The student was nervous before the test.* They might say *hands shaking, twisting a lock of hair, biting bottom lip, feeling butterflies in the stomach, swallowing hard,* and so forth. Writing in front of the class, the teacher could compose a sentence showing that the student was nervous before the test.

Example: Chewing on the end of his pencil, staring down at his test booklet, the student felt butterflies begin to take flight in his stomach, and he swallowed hard.

For writing warm-ups, the teacher could put a telling sentence up on the board for the students to work on, reminding them not to use the *telling* word in the sentence. For example:

The teenager was bored.
The birthday party was fun.
The blind woman was terrified of unfamiliar places.
She was very happy when the boy gave her a Valentine.

As students become more fluent and at ease with showing, not telling, they can form groups and compose telling sentences for other classmates to dramatize. Additionally, they can act these out in front of the class.

English learners may well understand the teacher's explanation of showing and not telling without themselves being able to show and not tell, largely because they are still learning the descriptive vocabulary and sentence structure to do so. They benefit from intensive vocabulary instruction that supports the lesson as well as from sentence-combining exercises related to incorporating modifiers, for example, including absolute phrases (word groups that modify entire sentences) such as, "The hikers rested before the fire, *their cold hands shaking in the frosty air*"; gerunds (verbals that function as nouns) such as "*Finding a needle in a haystack* would be easier than completing the marathon"; and participles, which are verbals used as adjectives and end in either -ed or –ing, such as "The crying child *screamed* for her mother" (-ed), or, "Teens interested in *studying* French should travel to France" (-ing). It should be noted that all these structures are challenging even for advanced English learners and should be taught in reasonable sets, usually one by one, over time. In general, they should not be presented together all at once, to avoid confusing or overwhelming students. ELs will have particular difficulty learning -ed and -ing participial forms (e.g., *interested* and *interesting*) when these forms are presented together and their meanings and uses not explained. Many ELs may not previously have been taught these forms and may be learning them for the first time.

Theme Collage Activity

Most narratives contain a theme—a lesson, message, or key idea that the writer wants to communicate to a reader. Although some writers directly state the theme, others convey the message more subtly, leaving the reader to make inferences and draw conclusions about the deeper meaning of the text. In other words, they might show the big idea through characters' actions, interactions, thoughts, and emotions rather than telling their reader what the point is. In a large-scale research study in an urban school district where 93% of the students speak English as their second language, students in grades 6–12 had great difficulty understanding, identifying, and analyzing theme—confusing theme with plot, character, setting, and topic (Olson, Land, Anselmi, & AuBuchon, 2010).

One way to help ELs understand what a theme is, is to characterize the topic of a narrative as the What and the theme as the So What? The teacher might explain this as follows:

A story's theme is different from its topic or subject. The topic is simply what it's about. The theme is the author's point about the topic. However, to identify a theme, sometimes it helps to generate a list of topics or big ideas in a story. Common topics for themes that you'll find in stories are usually abstract nouns that deal with human relationships and include terms like alienation, belonging, courage, family, friendship, hope, identity, prejudice, respect, revenge, trust, and so forth. Think of a topic as the What of the story and the theme as the So What? Therefore, a theme statement must be a complete sentence (with at least a subject and a verb) that states the author's message about life or about human relationships. A good theme statement applies to people in general, not just to the specific characters in the story. Here are some examples of theme statements:

Prejudice is a destructive force in our society.

Growing up means taking responsibility for yourself.

It is important to accept people for what they are on the inside and not the outside. (Olson, 2011, p. 342)

Next, students can be given a story to read, work collaboratively to identify a number of topic words that relate to the text, and then develop a theme statement that best expresses the message. Once they have articulated their theme statement, students can search through magazines or the Internet to find visuals that communicate their chosen themes. These visuals can be displayed as a collage along with the key topic words and the theme statement. Figure 3.6 includes a Theme Collage for "Eleven," by Sandra Cisneros, a story about a young girl and the humiliating experiences she faces on her 11th birthday.

Once ELs are better able to understand theme in the literary and nonfiction texts they read, they will have a clear idea of how to communicate a lesson, message, or key idea in their own narratives. Their teachers' scaffolding of challenging language features will help them succeed. English learners have special challenges communicating theme statements if they lack the vocabulary and grammatical structures to do so. Theme statements often involve using the dummy word *it* (as in *It is critical to understand people's true feelings*), which has no lexical meaning but does have a discoursegrammatical function, foregrounding information. Foregrounding is the practice of making words stand out from

Figure 3.6. Theme Collage

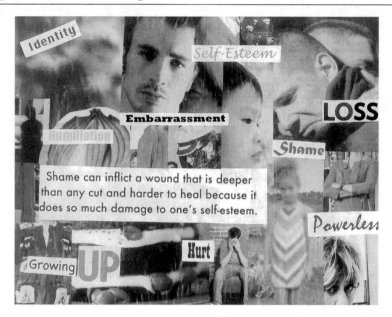

surrounding words. While using dummy subjects such as *there, it,* and *here* can make writing vague and unnecessarily wordy, dummy subjects are essential in a range of writing, and ELs can face challenges learning to use them if not instructed.

PUTTING IT ALL TOGETHER: WRITING NARRATIVES ABOUT *THE ARRIVAL*

In her sheltered English class attended by ELs in grades 9–12, Teresa Ozoa wanted to create an opportunity to put the minilessons she had taught her students about narrative writing to use by engaging them in giving voice to a rich and evocative wordless picture book called *The Arrival,* by author/illustrator Shaun Tan (2007), that she knew would resonate with them. This graphic novel, which resembles a weathered and worn family picture album, chronicles the story of an immigrant who leaves his native country under the shadow of some sinister threat in search of a new homeland for his family. Divided into six chapters, the book takes readers along with the protagonist on his journey, through his trials and tribulations as an outsider in a new and foreign environment and his ultimate assimilation. Tan, an Australian-born writer, strives to create empathy in his readers for the plight of his character. "In Australia," he remarks, "people don't stop to imagine what it's like for those refugees. They just see them as a problem once they're here, without thinking about the bigger picture. I don't expect the book to change anybody's opinion about things, but if it at least makes them pause and think, I'll feel as if I've succeeded in something" (Margolis, 2007).

Tan may have underestimated the power of his images. Through the universal immigration story they represent, Ozoa's students relived their own departures and arrivals and embraced the generosity and many kindnesses depicted in the book.

To begin the lesson, Ozoa introduced the idea of immigrants' dreams, especially coming to America, and asked her students to discuss their own hopes, expectations, and apprehensions before coming to the United States. Then, using a document camera, she engaged students in a picture walk through the book, calling upon students to access cognitive strategies, such as making predictions, tapping prior knowledge, forming interpretations, and reflecting and relating, as they constructed the gist of what was happening in each section of the book. For example, in the departure section of the story, the image of a dragon's tail haunts many of the pages. Students made an inference that some type of threat or menace was forcing the protagonist to flee his homeland. When the protagonist, a father who temporarily leaves his wife and daughter behind to seek a new life for the whole family, enters his new country in a port reminiscent of Ellis Island, he experiences difficulty communicating, finding housing, seeking food and a job, understanding the language, and so on. At this point, Ozoa asked students to do a quick write describing an event or emotion from the book they could relate to personally. For example, Jun Yamamoto wrote:

> The episode of the man having trouble to explain himself in the inspection at the immigration office reminded me of my experience when I first came to the United States. The pictures show the man tries to explain himself and his family in the inspection to enter the country, but he has trouble to explain and he looks very frustrated. When I came to the United States two years ago, I had trouble to answer the questions that were asked by an inspector and to explain myself since I couldn't speak English at all. I was really confused and frustrated that time because I couldn't say what I wanted to say and I was alone. The inspector looked scary and I could see a gun with

him. I was terrified by him and I literally couldn't speak. (Jun Yamamoto, 2014. Reprinted with permission)

Once they completed their visual journey through *The Arrival*, Ozoa placed students in small groups and asked them to select eight pages of their choice to bring to life by adding written narration, dialogue, interior monologue, action words, and sensory details. Students generated a first draft that they exchanged with another group of students who (1) highlighted in yellow all of the dialogue and interior monologue; (2) highlighted all of the sensory details in red; (3) wrote one compliment about the narrative; and (4) wrote one suggestion for improving the draft. Their finished narratives were published on the classroom bulletin board along with the pages from the book. The following is an excerpt from one group's work:

Jaffar was in a crowd of people trying to find a way or understand how he was supposed to get off the ship. When suddenly he realized that one of the crew members was saying, "Opp tip top gooz" and Jaffar thought to himself, "He must be pointing the way off the ship." The crew members opened the door and everybody got off the ship. After the travelers got their suitcases, the port was full of people. And they all found their way off the port. (Seyed Ali Hosseini, Arash Azarmehr, and Armin Abidnejad, 2014. Reprinted with permission)

Ozoa noted, "My students' narratives were surprisingly powerful and set the stage for a culminating unit I implemented on 'How to Achieve My American Dream.'"

English learners face many challenges in this Putting It All Together Narrative activity. Our analysis of EL students' quick write assignments pertaining to *The Arrival* reveals the most common language problems of ELs: sentence structure errors, verb tense mistakes, punctuation issues, and vocabulary.

WRITING THE PERSONAL NARRATIVE

Although the K–5 CCSS place an equal emphasis on narrative, informational, and argumentative writing, the percentage of narrative writing decreases in grades 6–12. As a result, the majority of narrative writing students compose is more likely to involve real experiences and events that are relevant to students' lives rather than purely fictional ones. Personal narratives usually include an element of reflection regarding the significance of what is "experienced, observed, or resolved over the course of the narrative" (National Governors Association, 2010, p. 16). What follows are three sample prompts for personal narrative writing that engage students in dramatizing significant events in their lives and reflecting upon their impact.

Prompt: The Memory Snapshot

Select a photograph that you associate with a significant memory. It can be a picture of you at any age, of another family member (or the whole family) or other significant person, of a vacation, or of an important event, a special place, and so on. (If you have a vivid mental snapshot inside your head that you do not have a photograph of but that you very much want to bring to life, this is OK.) Think about why you chose your snapshot—tangible and/or mental. How and why did the experience it depicts make a lasting impression on you?

Your task will be to create a written mental snapshot that captures your photograph in words and creates a *you are there* feeling in the reader. Use the magic camera of your pen to zoom in on your subject and pinpoint rich sensory details (sight, sound, smell, taste, touch, and movement). Remember that you can make your snapshot a "moving picture" by adding action and dialogue. Also, give the reader a more panoramic view of thoughts, feelings, and big ideas to create a frame for your specific details.

You will be writing an autobiographical incident account about your memory/snapshot. An autobiographical incident focuses on a specific time period and a particular event that directly involves you. Your goal is not to tell about your event but to show what happened by dramatizing the event. You may write in the present tense, as if your event were happening now, or in the past tense to describe your incident as a recollection.

Figure 3.7 presents a sample Memory Snapshot paper entitled "One Minute of Destruction" about the earthquake and tsunami in Japan in 2011, which an English learner composed in her sheltered English class and framed for the class Gallery Walk, where students read one another's narratives and place a Post-it® with a kind comment around the edges of the draft.

Figure 3.7. Memory Snapshot

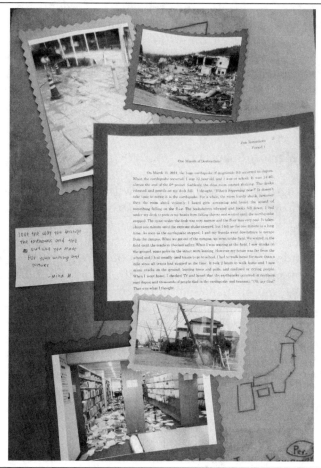

Source: Jun Yamamoto, 2014. Reprinted with permission.

Prompt: Watermarks

A watermark is a mark on a wall, building, or measuring stick indicating the height to which the water has risen. The mark could be the result of a regular, recurring motion as in the tides, or it could be made by a catastrophic event like a flood. In other words, a watermark is an event that has made a lasting impression.

Choose one of the important watermarks in your life that you would like to share with the class and the teacher. In a two- to three-page essay, first catch your reader's attention ("hook") and identify the watermark. Then describe the event that caused it, selecting important details to show the situation. Connect these with transitions. End your paper by explaining how this event is important to you today (Starbuck, in Olson, 1992).

Prompt: "When I Was Young in . . ." Narrative

After reading *When I Was Young in the Mountains*, by Cynthia Rylant (1982), a book that describes the author's childhood spent with her grandparents in Appalachia during the Great Depression, select a special memory from your childhood to write a narrative about. Emulating Rylant's style, repeat the phrase, "When I was young in . . ." throughout your narrative. Below is an excerpt from Moy Kiev Ung's reminiscence "When I was young in Phnom Penh" from an 8th-grade English language arts class taught by Liz Harrington:

> When I was young in Phnom Penh I went to the main river in front of the castle to watch firework. I would go around buying cotton candy or juicy spider snacks. I was also holding a pink balloon. When I was young in Phnom Penh I would go and catchs the little tadpoles at the small river and would later release it. When I was young in Phnom Penh I went riding elephant with my family in the park. The elephant was hairy and would eat the peanut I fed him. Its cries was so loud I had to cover my ears. (Moy Kiev Ung, 2014. Reprinted with permission)

BLENDING GENRES: THE SATURATION RESEARCH PAPER

The CCR Anchor Standards for Writing remind us that students "need to know how to combine elements of different kinds of writing—for example, to use narrative strategies within argument and explanation within narrative—to produce complex and nuanced writing" (p. 11). One way to help students blend genres and to meet the CCSS Research Standards is to ask students to conduct a historical investigation of a famous figure (artist, politician, sports hero, religious leader, scientist, etc.) and to select a pivotal event in that person's life to dramatize in a saturation research paper (D'Aoust, 1997). After researching the person and event and creating a one- to two-page expository summary of the event, students take on the persona and voice of that person and write a historical fiction in the first person, dramatizing the event in the character's own words. Students can write in the present tense, as if the events were happening now, or in the past tense as a recollection, but the point is to create a *you are there* feeling in the reader. To add an element of reflection to the historical fiction, students are challenged to show, and not tell, why that event was especially significant. The excerpt below includes the opening scene of Jennifer Cheng's Saturation Research Paper in Rachel Gorman's 9th-grade literature and composition class. The paper focuses on the execution of Anne Boleyn, followed by the beginning of the flashback of the events leading up to this "moment of awakening" narrated by King Henry VIII, including a citation from *The Love Letters of Henry VIII to Anne Boleyn* (Bach, 2010). Despite the obvious EL errors, this paper is remarkably sophisticated in its use of dialogue, interior monologue, flashback, and descriptive language.

Moment of Awakening

"You can say something to the audience before you die," one of the executioners said. It sounded like a command, not an announcement. Her long black hair covered her face, and her voice sounded hollow and sharp. "I can't accept the crime of which the kind and nobleman charged me. Even if I die, I curse the king forever," she said hoarsely.

"Enough!" the executioner stopped her. I watched as the executioner pressed her on the gallows and spit next to her. An uproar from the audience got louder and louder.

* * *

Anne Boleyn was a beautiful and mysterious girl. She didn't care about whom she talked with, but showed to others what she wanted, clearly and proudly. Too many women around me followed my leadership, said what I wanted to hear, or even betrayed their own minds, just because they wanted to get benefits from me.

I spent many months obsessed with Anne. After a while, I get used to writer letter to her. Then the writing of letters to Anne Boleyn became a habit. I received some what comfort by her letters. The words I chose became more specific and strong. I wrote quietly:

Dear Anne,

In turning over in my mind the contents of your last letters, I have put myself into great agony. Since I met you at the first time, I have been for above a whole year stricken with the dart of love, and not yet sure whether I shall fail of finding a place in your heart and affection. I beseech you to give me an entire answer to this my rude letter. No more, for fear of tiring you.

Ever yours,
H.R. (Henry VIII Letters)

Soon, Anne wrote back to me, but she didn't give me an answer. Day after day, I tried to ask her answer about being my mistress, but she just avoided the question. I couldn't endure this uncertain relationship anymore. I wrote a letter again,

Although, my mistress, it has not pleased you to remember the promise you made me when I was last with you—that is, to hear good news from you, and to have an answer to my last letter; yet it seems to me that it belongs to a true servant.

H.R. (Henry VIII Letters) (Jennifer Cheng, 2014. Reprinted with permission)

PROVIDING STUDENTS WITH FEEDBACK ON DRAFTS

When helping EL students edit their draft narratives, teachers will find it valuable to teach or review verb tense. Verb tense endings are difficult for students to hear in speech, because they are rarely pronounced clearly and sometimes EL students' classmates do not use endings in informal oral communication. Also, ELs often can communicate what they want to say without them. In narrative writing, verb tense can be especially tricky, since effective writers deliberately use verb tense in dialogues as it is used in oral language, to convey realistic communication that is representative of specific dialects. Moreover, they often switch to the literary present, for example, when introducing titles of literary works and when making evaluative statements and moral judgments in their concluding paragraphs. Teachers can teach verb tense using timelines and teaching only the key verb tenses that students need to use, reminding students to switch verb tenses only when they have an excellent reason for doing so. Helping students match verb tenses to time markers (like *now*, *yesterday*, and *last summer*) in their own and their classmates' writing is especially effective.

To Sum Up

- Narrative writing is a genre used to convey experience, either real or imagined, and serves many purposes, such as to inform, to instruct, to entertain, and to persuade.

- The Common Core State Standards for English Language Arts recommend that teachers spend anywhere from 35% of instructional time (in the primary grades) to 20% of instructional time (in the secondary grades) on teaching narrative writing.

- Narrative writing has tremendous potential in helping ELs develop their English proficiency and succeed in their coursework by leveraging their community knowledge and previous linguistic knowledge, including informal oral English, to express what they know, and it provides English teachers with a way to inventory the skills ELs have in reading and writing, build on student knowledge, and familiarize themselves with their students' cultures, communities, and experiences.

- Researchers emphasize the pivotal role narratives play in motivating students and building their confidence as writers by allowing them to write about meaningful experiences, reflect on these experiences, and bring them into perspective.

- Narrative writing also serves as a gateway to learning other types of writing, such as persuasive and report writing, as it helps students to develop audience awareness, organizational skills, and the ability to select and use specific and concrete details.

- Narrative writing contributes to students' ability to read literature critically and identify the particular techniques that would be useful in their own writing.

CHAPTER 4

Informative/Explanatory Texts and CCSS

Because of the importance of informative writing in a range of academic areas in all secondary grades, the CCSS for grades 6–12 emphasize the ability to write informative/explanatory texts. Such texts "examine and convey complex ideas and information clearly and accurately through the effective selection, organization, and analysis of content" (National Governors Association, 2010, p. 41). In other words, the writers' purpose is to teach their readers about a given topic with text-based details.

When students read informative/explanatory texts, they do so for an authentic purpose—to obtain information that they want or need to know (Purcell-Gates, Duke, Hall, & Tower, 2002). Informative/ explanatory writing enables them to understand the world around them, for example, to learn about topics ranging from diverse customs, to their pets' behaviors, to recent advances in medicine. Their success in schooling, the workplace, and society depends on their ability to read informational text and write about it (Duke, 2004). Informative/explanatory writing also leads to substantial opportunities to increase home–school–community connections (Duke & Purcell-Gates, 2003). Many ELs prefer this type of writing and are better at it than literary analyses or narratives. They are inspired when teachers invite them to write about nonfiction texts, newspapers, magazines, and reference books (Duke, Bennett-Armistead, & Roberts, 2002, 2003). They value their abilities to read some parts of informative text quickly and scan other parts, and to summarize their reading, discussions, and learning in writing and to write reports; they use these abilities routinely in many of their classes.

THE LANGUAGE DEMANDS OF INFORMATIVE/EXPLANATORY WRITING

Informational writing, the conveying of factual information about a nonfiction topic, uses impersonal, objective language (Schleppegrell,

2004). According to the CCSS, it includes procedural text and documentation. Examples include factual information and research reports; newspaper, magazine, and Internet articles; summaries; and brochures and pamphlets. Expository and informational writing often are linked because they have a common purpose—to share information or to inform others of an aspect of the social or natural world. Informational writing requires writers to synthesize information from multiple sources, some of which may be conflicting and need critical analysis (Shanahan & Shanahan, 2008). Characteristic text structures of informational text include descriptions, sequencing, compare/contrast, cause/effect, and problem/solution.

When organizing informational texts, writers often include a title, an introduction, a body, and a concluding section that summarizes their key points. They craft a clear statement that identifies their central purpose and present detailed factual information to make sure that their readers understand their topic. They use definitions and textual features like maps, timelines, photos or drawings, graphs, and tables to clarify their writing, and incorporate them appropriately into their texts when needed (Roberts et al., 2013). Their paragraphs begin with strong topic sentences linked in specific ways to the subject being discussed. Often, when writers introduce new concepts, they initially define them and then further elaborate on them, using examples and restatements. In so doing, they often use transition words like *for example, for instance, in fact, in other words,* and *hence.* In terms of language, they often use the timeless present tense to convey general truths. They use many academic words, like *survive,* which are used across subject areas, and use fewer everyday, commonly occurring words, like *live.*

English learners with moderate to strong levels of English proficiency often require instruction in the language resources needed to write informational text, especially when such text includes discipline-specific language and content. They benefit from in-depth instruction of the organizational features of informational text. ELs of this proficiency level are still acquiring the English modality system and may not be able to use a range of modal auxiliaries (*may, should, might*) to express thesis and topic sentences, and to express themselves with authority. They also require instruction in supporting key points, sentence complexity, pronoun reference, using transition words, cohesive devices, verb tense, and content-specific words and the academic words that support them. Learners at the emergent level of English proficiency may need similar instruction as well as instruction related to basic sentence and paragraph structure, nouns (plural and singular forms), verbs (especially verb tense), and content-specific and academic words. ELs, in general, benefit from instruction in word-learning strategies that help them become independent word learners (Baker et al., 2014).

INFORMATIONAL TALK TO READ AND WRITE INFORMATIONAL TEXTS

English learners often lack the academic language with which to convey information in a school context. One way to help them acquire language to instruct, test, summarize, compare and contrast, analyze, and so forth, is to have them use sentence stems to orally rehearse the use of academic vocabulary before they apply it to their writing. Students are first given an opportunity to build their knowledge about a topic of special interest (how to score a goal in soccer, the newest "apps" for their mobile devices, the aftermath of the 2011 tsunami in Japan, the merits of their favorite musical group, whether McDonalds or Burger King makes the best french fries, etc.). After students research their chosen topics, recording interesting facts and sequencing their ideas, they are given 20 minutes to share their findings with a partner. Prior to their discussions, the teacher models a topic of his or her own, using appropriate sentence starters such as: *The factors that are the most important are . . . ; X and Y are similar because . . . ; To summarize the main points of this discussion, I believe we have said . . .* As one partner holds forth, the other partner asks questions as well as records any academic words he or she heard the partner use. This oral rehearsal can precede the composition of a formal paper on the student's area of interest.

While building oral language skills is important for all students, it is even more so for ELs (Harper & Jong, 2004). This is especially the case when writing informative text. In this type of writing, students often read complex texts and complete collaborative writing assignments. Their doing so often calls on them to read critically, cooperate with one another when writing, use large vocabularies and complex grammatical structures, and form independent conclusions. A number of educators concur that thoughtfully constructed oral language activities contribute to the development of such abilities (Baker et al., 2014; Goldenberg, 2012; van Lier & Walqui, 2012). They also agree that writing and oral language have an interrelated and complex relationship.

However, ELs often have few opportunities to talk in class in ways that enable them to use oral language as a rehearsal to writing (Williams, Stathis, & Gotsch, 2009). It is important to note that not all student talk benefits ELs' writing development. When ELs use only informal "student talk" with their classmates, they do not develop the language they need to communicate in many types of informative writing assignments.

TEACHING TEXT STRUCTURES TO READ AND WRITE INFORMATIONAL TEXTS

In *Get It Done! Writing and Analyzing Informational Texts to Make Things Happen*, Wilhelm, Smith, and Fredricksen (2012) remark:

> We've come to see that informative/explanatory texts are, at their heart, different ways to categorize. What this means is that each informational text type requires a different and very particular kind of thought. *That is, each kind of informational text structure embodies a specific way of thinking with and through categories.* In turn, this means that teaching students how to understand, produce, and use informational text structures means that we are teaching them how to think with specific categorical patterning tools. (p.11, emphasis in the original)

Let's take a look at five text structures that commonly appear in informative/explanatory texts (Meyer, 1985, 2003).

Description

The purpose of this text structure is to tell what something is, to present an item's attributes or properties, to show what an item or place is like, and to help readers visualize what is being described. In this organizational pattern, a topic is described by listing characteristics, features, and examples. Phrases such as *for example* and *characteristics are* cue this structure.

Sequence

This pattern is used to show how to do something or make something, or to relate a series of events that happen over time. Items or events are listed or explained in numerical or chronological order.

Cue words for sequence include *first, second, third, next, then,* and *finally.*

Comparison/Contrast

In the comparison/contrast structure, two or more things are compared to show how they are alike or contrasted to show how they are different. *Different, in contrast, alike,* and *on the other hand* are cue words and phrases that signal this structure.

Cause/Effect

Writers use this structure to show why something exists or is in place, to tell what happens as the result of an action or actions, or to show how one or more causes lead to effects. *If . . . then, as a result, therefore,* and *because* all signal a cause/effect structure, as does *reasons why.*

Problem/Solution

In this expository structure, the writer states a problem and offers one or more solutions. Cue words and phrases include *the problem is, the puzzle is, solve,* and *question . . . answer.*

Researchers have confirmed that when students use the five expository text structures to organize their reading and writing, they are more effective readers and writers (Langer, 1986; Raphael, Englert, & Kirschner, 1989; Tompkins, 2013). Figure 4.1 contains a chart of the text structures, including the pattern, description, cue or signal words associated with each text type, a graphic organizer that lends itself to the underlying structure, and a sample paragraph about the topic of tsunamis.

One effective inductive method to either introduce students to the five text structures or provide practice after the teacher has explicitly introduced each one is to recreate the chart in Figure 4.1 with only the pattern and description columns filled in and the other columns left blank, and then to copy the original chart; cut up the cue words, graphic organizers, and sample passages; and place them into envelopes. Students are then asked to work in pairs and use glue sticks to reconstruct the chart, using the items in the envelope, without the teacher's assistance. The next step after the chart has been completed is for students to compare their versions with the master version. To reinforce this practice, the teacher can give

Figure 4.1. The Five Expository Text Structures

Pattern	Description	Cue Words	Graphic Organizer	Sample Passage
Description	The author describes a topic by listing characteristics, features, and examples	*characteristics* *are, features* *are, for* *example*		Tsunami is a Japanese word used to describe a seismic sea wave or a series of large ocean waves with extremely long wavelengths and long periods. A tsunami may travel hundreds of miles across the deep ocean, reaching speeds up to 500–600 miles an hour. For example, a tsunami initiated by an earthquake off the coast of Alaska can travel within a few hours across the Pacific and threaten the Hawaiian Islands. Upon entering shallow coastal waters, the wave, which may have been only about a foot or two high out at sea, suddenly begins growing rapidly. By the time it reaches the shore, it may become a towering wall of water 50 feet high or more, capable of destroying thousands of lives and obliterating entire coastal settlements.

Source: Tompkins, Gail E. Literacy For the 21st Century: A Balanced Approach, 6th Ed., © 2014. Printed and electronically reproduced by permission of Pearson Education, Inc., Upper Saddle River, New Jersey.

Figure 4.1. The Five Expository Text Structures (continued)

Pattern	Description	Cue Words	Graphic Organizer	Sample Passage
Sequence	The author lists items or events in numerical or chronological order.	*first, second, third, next, then, finally*	1. _____ 2. _____ 3. _____ 4. _____ 5. _____	A tsunami typically goes through four stages. The first phase, "Initiation," occurs with the event that triggers the beginning of a tsunami, usually an undersea earthquake. The next stage is the "Split." Within several minutes of the earthquake, the initial tsunami is split into one that travels out to the deep ocean (distant tsunami) and another that travels toward the nearby coast (local tsunami). After the tsunami splits, the third stage, "Amplification," occurs. As the local tsunami approaches the shore, its amplitude (height) increases. At the same time, the wavelength decreases. When the deep ocean, distant tsunami approaches land, amplification and shortening of the wave also will occur, just as with the local tsunami. The final stage of a tsunami is the "Runup." It occurs when a peak in the tsunami wave travels from the near-shore region onto shore. Most tsunamis do not result in giant waves, but instead come in much like very strong and fast-moving tides.

Source: Tompkins, Gail E. Literacy For the 21st Century: A Balanced Approach, 6th Ed., © 2014. Printed and electronically reproduced by permission of Pearson Education, Inc., Upper Saddle River, New Jersey.

Figure 4.1. The Five Expository Text Structures (continued)

Pattern	Description	Cue Words	Graphic Organizer	Sample Passage
Comparison and Contrast	The author explains how two or more things are alike and/or how they are different.	*Different, in contrast, alike, same as, on the other hand*	Alike Different	While regular ocean waves and tsunamis share a few similarities, they also have some obvious differences. Both are a mode of energy transfer and can be described by their wavelength, speed, frequency, period, amplitude (height), and energy. In addition, shoaling, increasing in height when entering shallow water, is common to both regular waves and tsunamis. However, regular waves and tsunamis have several important differences. Whereas regular waves are caused primarily by wind, tsunamis are most often the result of undersea earthquakes. Normal ocean waves are a surface feature and the water beneath the surface is barely affected. In contrast, tsunamis propagate through the entire depth of the ocean. While regular waves cannot go further than a mile, tsunamis can traverse the entire earth. Of course, the obvious difference between the two types of waves is their size. Regular waves have a wavelength of a few meters at best. On the other hand, tsunamis can have wavelengths of over a hundred miles and are capable of causing untold damage.

Source: Tompkins, Gail E. Literacy For the 21st Century: A Balanced Approach, 6th Ed., © 2014. Printed and electronically reproduced by permission of Pearson Education, Inc., Upper Saddle River, New Jersey.

Figure 4.1. The Five Expository Text Structures (continued)

Pattern	Description	Cue Words	Graphic Organizer	Sample Passage
Cause and Effects	The author lists one or more causes and the resulting effect or effects.	*reasons why, if . . . then, as a result, therefore , because*	Cause → Effect1, Effect2, Effect3	Tsunamis are some of the most devastating natural disasters known to humanity. One reason why they are so treacherous is that their powerful waves can move up to 600 miles per hour and destroy even well-built structures when they pound the coastline. Another effect of tsunamis is their cost to human life. The deadliest tsunamis in recorded history were the Christmas tsunamis of 2004 in the Indian Ocean. A 9.2 earthquake occurred off the island of Sumatra and created a deadly series of tsunamis that swept Indonesia, India, Madagascar, and Ethiopia. The death toll was estimated to be over 230,000. Even after the tsunamis have passed and the waters have retreated, the stagnation of the water causes contamination of the clean drinking water supply, resulting in sickness and death among the survivors.

Source: Tompkins, Gail E. Literacy For the 21st Century: A Balanced Approach, 6th Ed., © 2014. Printed and electronically reproduced by permission of Pearson Education, Inc., Upper Saddle River, New Jersey.

Figure 4.1. The Five Expository Text Structures (continued)

Pattern	Description	Cue Words	Graphic Organizer	Sample Passage
Problem and Solution	The author states a problem and lists one or more solutions for the problem. A variation of this pattern is the question-and-answer format in which the author poses a question and then answers it.	*problem is, dilemma is, puzzle is solved, question . . . answer*	Problem → Solution	Throughout history, tsunamis have been among the worst natural disasters. They are capable of causing untold damage and taking countless lives. In fact, in the Indian Ocean tsunami of 2004, over 230,000 people lost their lives. Unfortunately, since there is no way to eliminate tsunamis, we must look for ways to minimize their impact. One solution is to plan ahead with emergency measures and evacuation plans and routes. In addition, we need to conduct more research to improve the present early warning devices. Also, communities need to build more secure structures, preferably on higher ground. A final solution would be to construct sea walls and barrier reefs in vulnerable areas.

Source: Tompkins, Gail E. Literacy For the 21st Century: A Balanced Approach, 6th Ed., © 2014. Printed and electronically reproduced by permission of Pearson Education, Inc., Upper Saddle River, New Jersey.

students a nonfiction text such as one about another natural disaster like a hurricane, tornado, or earthquake and ask them to identify the text structures the author has used. This practice will set the stage for ELs to begin to use these structures in their own writing.

It is especially beneficial for ELs to learn text structures. In reading, these structures allow students to understand the organization of informational texts and make sense of their content. In writing, they permit students to manage the cognitively and linguistically complex task of composing, helping them to organize their thoughts effectively (Graham & Perin, 2007). Since ELs may be cognitively overloaded, especially when completing writing assignments in classrooms in which they are held to the same performance standards as more proficient English-speaking classmates (Short & Fitzsimmons, 2007), they may feel challenged to retrieve words and language structures while at the same time getting their ideas down in an organized fashion. Understanding text structures can reduce their linguistic, cognitive, and affective constraints, building their self-confidence as writers and buying them time to write.

However, text organization also poses challenges for ELs. They may be unfamiliar with specific text types because they have never been exposed to them or never received instruction in their use. Further, those who received reading and writing instruction in their primary languages in their home countries may not be familiar with the text structures used in the United States, and they may draw upon their knowledge of structures from their primary languages when writing informational texts in English. Since different cultures value different ways of organizing informational text, ELs' text organization may reflect language transfer. In today's global world, Western structures of text organization are taught, albeit to varying degrees, in national curricula across the world, including those of Mainland China (Ministry of Education of the People's Republic of China, 2011). Therefore, it behooves ELs to learn these structures.

Each text structure holds specific challenges for ELs. To use the *description* text structure, for example, ELs may benefit from instruction on the content that they should include in their descriptions and explanations of where to put this content. Some may find it challenging to avoid summarizing what they have said. They may not know figurative language and sensory words and the types of empathetic responses that they yield, or may not have the words to express moment-to-moment details. Writing text using the *sequencing* structure also challenges ELs. They may lack the experience required to use this structure to give directions pertaining to specific tasks, and they may switch between imperative and declarative statements in inappropriate ways. In terms of the *comparison/contrast* text structure, ELs may not know how to make adjectives into comparison forms with -er and -est endings and *more* and *most*. They may not understand that the word *with* follows *compared* in the sentence, "Compared with last year's earthquake, the 2010 earthquake was not severe." Instead, they may write, "Comparing to last year's earthquake, the 2010 earthquake was not severe." Even more challenging for ELs is the *cause/effect* text structure and its associated word demands. They are still in the process of learning verbs and nouns related to causation that collocate with prepositions, and they may be confused because while the verb *sometimes* does not take a preposition, the noun does. We say, "X affects Y," but "X has an effect on Y." Along similar lines, ELs may not know the verbs that can indicate causation (e.g., *affect, cause, contribute to, create, develop, give rise to, influence, lead to, result from, stem from*, and *trigger*), so teachers will want to teach these verbs. The *problem/solution* text structure is particularly problematic for ELs because even ELs with advanced English proficiency may lack the ability to use modal auxiliaries like *can, may,* and *must* to mitigate the strength of their words or to weigh the value of one solution compared with another.

TEACHING SEQUENCING:
THE PEANUT BUTTER AND JELLY SANDWICH ACTIVITY

Sequencing, whether it involves steps in a process, stages of an event, reasons for a cause or effect, or identifying items in a series, is an important feature of informational writing. After introducing sequence words like *first, next, then, after that*, and *finally*, the teacher can model sequencing by demonstrating how to do something while consulting with the class regarding what to do in what order. This also will give students an opportunity to practice the CCSS Speaking and Listening Standards. One popular "how to" activity in ELD classrooms is to demonstrate how to make a peanut butter and jelly sandwich, following directions provided by the class. To begin, the teacher assembles the jars of peanut butter and jelly, the bread, plate, and knife on a table at the front of the room. She might ask students whether they ever had to give directions to someone and whether that person clearly understood their instructions. She then appeals to the class for help in making a peanut butter and jelly sandwich, insisting that she will follow their instructions to the letter. For example, if a student says, "Put the peanut butter on the bread," but fails to tell the teacher to open the jar, she will place the entire jar on the bread. She might ask, "What do I need to do first in order to get the peanut butter out?" If after telling the teacher to open the jar, they simply say, "Now spread the peanut butter on the bread," without instructing her to use a knife, she may put her fingers in the jar. Although much laughter will ensue, the students do learn a valuable lesson. Once the teacher has accomplished the task using the students' verbal directions, she can ask them to individually write down directions. They can then take turns having one student up front trying to make the sandwich according to the written directions provided by a partner. When using the sequencing text structure, ELs often have difficulty using transition words to link ideas appropriately. The teacher can ask students to complete a cloze activity such as the one in Figure 4.2 to practice using transition words.

When they have completed this activity, students can examine their own instructions and search for transition words, circling each one that they find. They can then revise their own writing using transition words effectively. The peanut butter and jelly or other teacher-guided sequencing activity can lead to a more extended "how to" assignment where students write out instructions for how to do something (e.g., build a skateboard ramp, make a pie, score a soccer goal, play a video game), which they demonstrate in front of the class.

THE OREOS AND FIG NEWTONS
COMPARISON/CONTRAST TEXT STRUCTURE ACTIVITY

English learners often have difficulty comparing and contrasting because they have not yet learned comparative adjectives and structures. One way to make this text structure more accessible is to begin with something very concrete. Just as the peanut butter and jelly activity can help ELs to grasp cue words for sequencing and to logically order instructions, the Oreos and Fig Newtons activity can make comparing and contrasting memorable and fun. Actually, any variety of cookies will do, as will objects like seashells, flowers, or shoes.

The teacher can commence the lesson by telling students that they will learn to compare and contrast and, at the same time, get to taste test cookies. To generate student interest, the teacher can ask

Figure 4.2. Cloze Activity: How to Make a Peanut Butter and Jelly Sandwich

Find the Transition Words

Transition words have been left out of the following paragraph. Select appropriate words from the list below, and write them in the proper places. There can be more than one word that fits in some places. Select the one that you think fits best.

How to Make a Peanut Butter and Jelly Sandwich

Word Bank: *Hence*   *However*   *Otherwise*
     As a consequence   *Alternatively*   *After this*

There are several steps to follow when making a peanut butter and jelly sandwich. The first and most important step is selecting your ingredients and gathering them together. Before you start, you will want to gather a kitchen knife, bread (usually one or two slices per sandwich), peanut butter, and jelly or jam. There are many different kinds of bread to choose from. _____, you will have to do a little experimenting to select the bread you like. After you have gathered all your ingredients, spread the peanut butter on the bread. You will probably want to spread it evenly. You may want to stir it before you spread it. _____ it may be lumpy. _____, spread the jelly on the other piece of bread. (_____ you can use jam.) Don't put too much on your bread or you will not be able to taste the peanut butter. After this, press the two pieces of bread together, but don't press too hard. _____, you may end up making a mess and destroying your sandwich. Next, cut the sandwich diagonally. After you have done this, you are ready to enjoy your sandwich.

---

students to brainstorm the qualities of their favorite cookie, including types, shapes, ingredients, and so forth. A word bank with vocabulary (e.g., *chocolate chip, crunchy, sweet, animal-shaped, ginger, round*) can be posted and added to throughout the lesson. Next, students can taste-test several cookies (such as Animal Crackers, Oreos, and Fig Newtons), selecting words from the word bank to describe the taste, smell, texture, and so on, and use their notes to generate "I like [Oreos, Animal Crackers, Fig Newtons] because ___" sentences. For example, a student might write, "I like Oreos because they are crispy and chocolatey on the outside and have a creamy, white filling on the inside." Then, the teacher can ask students to examine two different cookies and can present the following frame:

Both _____ and _____ are _____. However, _____ are _____ whereas _____ are _____. On the one hand, _____ and _____ are similar because _____. On the other hand, they are different because _____. Although _____, I personally like _____ better because _____.

To help students to complete the frame, the teacher can compare and contrast two other cookies. For example, the teacher might write:

> Both Famous Amos cookies and Animal Crackers are sweet and delicious. However, Famous Amos cookies are famous for the chocolate chips whereas Animal Crackers are frosted and have sprinkles. On the one hand, Famous Amos cookies and Animal Crackers are similar because they are small and bite-sized. On the other hand, they are different because one is round and the other is shaped like different animals. Although it's hard to resist Famous Amos cookies, I like Animal Crackers better because it is fun to swallow elephants and lions.

This type of rehearsal can precede strictly informative/explanatory writing such as comparing and contrasting two phenomena like tornadoes and thunderstorms, or it can become more analytical and open-ended such as comparing and contrasting literary characters like Katniss Everdeen in *The Hunger Games* by Suzanne Collins (2008) and Beatrice Prior in *Divergent* by Veronica Roth (2011). Comparison/contrast writing also can lead to argumentative writing if students are asked to form an opinion regarding which of the subjects being compared/contrasted is superior, preferable, the bravest, most hateful, least or most at fault for something, and so forth.

INTRODUCING ENGLISH LEARNERS TO INFORMATIONAL/ EXPOSITORY WRITING THROUGH THE PODCAST ACTIVITY

In his English language development class, which serves high school students with levels of English proficiency from newcomer to early intermediate, Stephen Hochschild wanted to introduce students to the CCSS writing standard for informational texts: Introduce a topic; organize complex ideas, concepts, and information to make important connections and distinctions; include formatting (e.g., headings), graphics (e.g., figures, tables), and multimedia when useful to aiding comprehension. Since his students speak Portuguese, Spanish, Korean, Farsi, Vietnamese, Mandarin, Taiwanese, and more, and are often unfamiliar with one another's home countries and customs, he decided to introduce students to informative/explanatory reading and writing in a way that would draw upon their own experiences and knowledge base. He prompted them to read expository texts, write a brief descriptive essay, create a PowerPoint, and deliver a speech that would be made available as a podcast in response to this prompt: "What is the best city in your country to visit and why? Be sure to include details about places to go, things to do, places to stay, how to get there, and any other information you think is important." Students used a variety of technology for the project, including PowerPoint, an iPhone recording app, GarageBand for the podcast, and expedia.com and other trip planning websites.

Figure 4.3 shows the writing and presentation template that Hochschild developed to guide students through the process. Note that it includes a few important words and phrases in each student's native language, which the student would teach the class during the presentation. In addition, students had to research the total cost of the trip and provide detailed instructions for how to get to their destinations. Since his students were still developing writers, Hochschild wrote a sample speech about San Francisco as a mentor text that students could consult and emulate. Figure 4.4 presents a sample student speech.

To culminate the project, Hochschild asked students to write again to the same prompt in an on-demand timed situation, allowing them to use dictionaries but none of their previous notes. He noticed that they were able to retain the structure of their podcast speeches and even added additional details and descriptive language. In the future, he plans to expand the unit to include the production of a travel brochure. Student engagement in the unit was very high and helped him cultivate a community of learners who gained respect for one another's cultures.

SUMMARY WRITING ACTIVITIES

Through summary writing activities, ELs can develop the sophisticated, abstract language necessary to give readers an accurate, objective, complete, and concise view of a piece of writing. English learners have particular challenges citing key details pertinent to

Figure 4.3. Writing and Presentation Template: ELD City Visit Presentation Writing

Below is the text sample for your presentation. You may describe more but this is your foundation.

Introduction/Title Page

Hello everyone, let me tell you about (City, Country). It is a/an _____ place!

Adjective (beautiful, wonderful, etc.)

Where is your country?

_____ is located near _____ in _____.
(Your country)   (Neighbor country) (Continent/Ocean)

Where is your city?

It is in the _____ of _____.
(North, south, east, west) (Country)

Basic facts about the city

_____ is _____, and it is famous for _____.
(City)   (Adjective)   (One famous aspect)

Basic facts about the country

It is interesting to know that _____ has a population of _____.
(Country)   (Population)
The main language is _____.
(Country language)
In addition, the main _____ is _____.
(Religion, art, craft, sport, etc.) (Write the name)

Important phrases

A few important phrases are the following: _____.
(Word or phrase)
Which means _____. [plus two phrases]
(Definition)

Places to visit

Some great places to visit in _____ are _____, _____, and _____.
(City)   (Interesting place #1, #2, #3)

_____ is known for _____. It costs _____ dollars. [Repeat for each place] *(Why it is famous)   (Cost)*
(Place)

Figure 4.3. Writing and Presentation Template: ELD City Visit Presentation Writing (continued)

Things to do ($)

Some exciting things to do are _____, _____, and _____.
(Exciting things to do)

_____ is exciting because it is _____. It costs _____ dollars.
(Thing to do)   *(Why it is fun)*   *(Cost)*

Best hotel ($)

The best hotel in _____ is _____. It is _____. It costs _____ dollars a night.

(Cost)   *(City)*   *(Hotel)*   *(Adjective)*

Best restaurant ($)

The best restaurant in _____ is _____. It is _____, and you can eat _____ there.

    (Popular food)   *(City)*   *(Restaurant)*   *(Adjective)*

It costs _____ dollars for _____ per person.

    (Cost)   *(Breakfast, lunch, dinner)*

Total cost of vacation ($$$)

This is a great vacation, and I believe you should visit! The total cost of the vacation is _____ dollars.

    (Total cost)

How to get there (airport/transportation)

To visit _____, fly to _____ and then take a _____ to _____. *(City)*

(City)   *(Airport)*   *(Bus, taxi, train)*

(City)

Please visit _____!

    (City, Country)

Source: Stephen Hochschild, 2014. Reprinted with permission.

their readings, recognizing central ideas, and emphasizing them appropriately. To help students summarize, a teacher might "anchor" her instruction in a common shared experience. For instance, she could use a brief 5-minute video and brief reading related to students' informative essay assignment (e.g., a video on Rosa Parks and the Civil Rights Movement) to build shared background knowledge. After viewing the video, both she and her students can "explain why a given fact or piece of information is important, and why other pieces of information are less important" (Baker et al.,

Figure 4.4. Sample Student Speech: Monterrey, Nuevo León, México

Hello everyone. Let me tell you about Monterrey, in México. It is a beautiful and exciting place! Monterrey is located next to Coahulila in México. It is the north of México. Monterrey is beautiful, cultural, and it is famous for The Saddle Hill (El Cerro de la Silla).

It is interesting to know that México has a population of about 12.3 million people. The main language is Spanish, but in some states they speak English too. In addition, the main national religion is Catholicism.

A few important phrases are the following: 'Hola' which means 'Hi/ Hello,' '¿Hablas _____?' which means 'Do you speak _____?' and '¿Sabes donde esta _____?' Which means 'Do you know where _____ is it?' these phrases will help in Monterrey!

Some great places to visit in Monterrey are Plaza Sesamo, Paseo Santa Lucía, Bioparque Estrella, La Arena Monterrey, La Macroplaza, El Barrio Antiguo, La Cola de Caballo, Las Grutas de García and La Presa de la Boca. Plaza Sesamo and Bioparque Estrella are amusement parks, however El Paseo Santa Lucía, El Barrio Antiguo are free places, you can walk around and see diferent monuments, La Cola de caballo and Las Grutas de García are a turist places, the people whom live in Monterrey can go too, but those places are famous and are so pretty, La Macroplaza is known becaue there are a lot of different Shop Stores, at last La Arena Monterrey are known for the big events like 'Book Fair' and events like that.

Some exciting things to do are riding the cable car in Las Grutas de García, shopping in La Macroplaza and do some ejercise in El Paseo Santa Lucía. The Cable Car is exciting because you can see all the people walking below you (they look like ants). It costs about 10 dollars. Going to buy wherever you want in La Macroplaza are awesome. It costs about 20 dollars. Finally, do some ejercise in El Paseo Santa Lucía is healthy and unique, it is fee, so you can go whenever you want.

The best hotel in Monterrey is the Safi Royal Luxury Hotel. It is elegant and inside is very big and comfortable. It costs about 160 dollars per night. The Safi is located in San Pedro Garza García, the most expensive, safety and rich part of Monterrey.

The best restaurant in Monterrey is Yamoto. It is delicious and elegant, and you can eat delicious Japanese food there. It costs about 30 or 35 dollars per person. Everyone raves about it!

This is a great vacation, and I believe you should visit! The total cost of the vacation is about $300 dollars.

To visit Monterrey, fly to Monterrey International Airport, and then take a bus of taxi to your hotel. Please visit Monterrey, Nuevo León in México!

Source: Barbara Alvarez, 2014. Reprinted with permission.

2014, p. 32). ELs, in particular, benefit from the explicit guidelines provided below for composing written summaries.

When writing a summary, follow these steps:

1. Read the original text and make sure that you understand the main ideas. The author's thesis and the topic sentences often will give you clues. Do not be distracted by minor details.
2. Outline your text on a separate sheet of paper without looking back at the original text. Use key words and phrases.
3. Choose the main idea from your outline to be the topic of the first sentence of your summary. This sentence should contain the central idea of the original text, the title and date of the text, and the author's full name. If the article appears in a magazine, newspaper, or book, include the name of the magazine, newspaper, or book. The first time you refer to the author, use the author's first and last name. After that, refer to the author by his or her last name only.
4. Decide on the appropriate order for the rest of the information in your outline. You may wish to organize the information in a different order than how it appears in the original text.
5. Without referring to the original text, write out your summary in your own words. Do not plagiarize! Use only words, phrases, and grammatical structures that you understand. Your summary should include all the elements of formal, academic writing.

It is also important to remind students to write in the present tense. Additionally, the teacher may want to require students to incorporate one quotation from the text into their summaries.

To prepare ELs for the writing task, the teacher can ask students to work in small groups to complete a graphic organizer outlining the writer's main topics and issues covered in the reading. She can circulate among the students and ask, "What do you think the main idea in this paragraph is?" and assist them in ordering the importance of the points the author makes. To provide oral practice in summarizing before the students summarize in writing, she can have students practice asking one another questions about the relevance of specific pieces of information in their passages. The following sentence starters can help ELs use their graphic organizers to summarize their reading in writing:

Sentence Frames for Summary

The writer discusses _____ and explores issues of _____.

The writer argues that _____ and illustrates the point by emphasizing that _____.

In summary, the author explores issues of _____ and explains to the reader that _____ is important because _____.

ELs find checklists, such as the one in Figure 4.5, for summary writing helpful, especially in peer reviews.

THE SATURATION REPORT/ACTIVITY: HELPING ENGLISH LEARNERS BECOME INVESTIGATIVE JOURNALISTS

One assignment that introduces students to informative/explanatory writing and draws on students' sensory/descriptive and narrative strengths, while also preparing them for more complex, analytical research writing, is the saturation report. Popularized by National Writing Project teacher/consultant Ruby Bernstein (Olson, 1997), the saturation report draws from Tom Wolfe's concept of "new journalism" and encourages students to practice observing, interviewing, separating fact from opinion, and conducting both first- and sometimes secondhand research as they report on real people, places, or events. As described by Bernstein, the key features of a saturation report are as follows:

Writing about some place, some event, some group, or some individual that you know well or can get to know well firsthand. You "saturate" yourself with your subject.

Writing a nonfiction article, using fictional techniques. There will be scenes, characters and characterizations, dialogue, and a subtle, rather than overt, statement.

The appeal of information and facts. You are writing nonfiction, and the reader will want to "know" about your subject; in short, be sensitive to this thirst for facts on the part of your reader.

Figure 4.5. Checklist for Summary

Name of writer: _____
Name of reviewer: _____

Important Details

__ Title and date of the original text and the author's full name are in the first sentence.

__ Author is referred to by last name only after the first sentence.

__ Title of the original text is in quotation marks, NOT italicized or underlined.

__ Author's thesis and main points are in the first sentences.

__ Summary is written in the present tense.

__ Summary is appropriate length (150–200 words).

Comments

Yes No 1. Does the writer clearly state the author's main point and supporting points?

Yes No 2. Does the writer omit unnecessary details?

Yes No 3. Does the summary contain the writer's opinion?

Yes No 4. Does the summary read smoothly and use transitions?

Yes No 5. Does the writer mention the author's name more than one time?
        If yes, how many times? _____

1. What verbs does the writer use to introduce the author's ideas/opinions/ thesis? (For example, *Smith says/states/believes/asserts/ suggests/ criticizes* . . .) List them below.

_____

2. Does the writer include one quotation from the original text and explain it? Yes No

   *If yes, does the writer follow these three steps for integrating a quotation?

   Yes No   Step 1: <u>Introduce the quotation</u> using a signal phrase such as:

              Smith says or *He claims that* . . .

   Yes No   Step 2: <u>Give the quotation</u> using proper punctuation.

              (Commas and periods go inside quotation marks.)

Figure 4.5. Checklist for Summary (continued)

Yes No   Step 3: <u>Follow up the quotation</u> with a sentence that explains it or comments on it.

3. Would a reader of the summary who had not read the original text get a clear idea of the text? Explain.

_____
_____
_____
_____

4. Other Comments:

_____
_____
_____
_____
_____

Author identification. Your point of view can be quite flexible. You can be an active participant in the action; you can remove yourself; or you can come in and then move out.

Microcosm. You are focusing on some particular subject, but in so doing you are saying something more. As you capture an isolated segment of today's world, you say something about the total world.

Implication. Much of what you attempt to "say" in your article (because of your use of fictional techniques) will be said through implication—through dialogue and through your manipulation of details.

Reporting. You will observe your subject with a keen eye. You will note interesting "overheard" conversations. You might want to interview someone.

Form. You might write your article in pieces—conversations, descriptions, interviews, facts—and then piece it together, finding the best form for your subject (time sequence and so forth). A "patchwork"—working sections together with no transition—can be quite acceptable.

Choice of subject. You can pick some subject from the present or recreate some subject from your past. (p. 138)

Using Bernstein's criteria as a foundation, the following sequence of activities can guide students through writing a saturation report:

Step 1. Explain to students several weeks in advance (so they have some "think time") that they will have an opportunity to immerse themselves in a person, place, or event and bring their subject to life by presenting factual information scene by scene, using description, characterization, dialogue, and so forth. Pass out the list of key features of a saturation report, as outlined by Ruby Bernstein. Brainstorm possible subjects for investigation. These might include places, events, or groups in your local area (Jenny Craig weight loss store, swap meet, chili cook-off, soccer game, political rally, etc.). But they also might include events that are particular to a cultural group (Quinceañera, Norooz [Persian New Year], Little Saigon, Cinco de Mayo, Tour de France, etc.).

Step 2. Provide students with a model of a saturation report and a list of criteria on which their papers will be evaluated. (This rubric should be created by each teacher to fit his or her objectives and classroom situation.) One student sample, a report on female mud wrestling written by Dave Meltzer, is available on the Internet (wps.ablongman.com/wps/media/objects/133/136299/stumodel.pdf).

Step 3. Once students have a clear idea of what the saturation report entails, ask them to brainstorm topics they could write about and to place the names on a chart with categories for people, places, and events, and then to select the topic they are most interested in.

Step 4. The students are now ready to go out and observe their person, place, or event. Encourage them to record everything they hear, see, touch, smell, taste, and so on, and to note their own impressions and reactions. Figure 4.6 is helpful for showing students what to record.

Step 5. When students come back to class with their notes, help them organize their ideas by asking them to think of themselves as photographers or cinematographers. If they were filming this, what kind of camera angles would they use? What focus? What kind of lighting? How often would they change the scene? Then ask them to create a scene-by-scene cluster of their report. Walk around the room to review these and offer suggestions.

Figure 4.6. Sensory Table

Writing Type	Record
Sensory/Descriptive	Sights, smells, tastes, textures, sounds, action words, character description
Imaginative/Narrative	Dialogue, time frame, ideas for scenes, transition words, dramatic effects, mood
Informative/Explanatory	Historical background, interesting facts and statistics, "how to" information, interview questions and responses
Analytical/Argument	First impressions, reactions, afterthoughts, opinions, judgments, criticisms

Step 6. To make sure the students are off to a good start, have them write their opening scene and bring copies to class for sharing.

To scaffold the saturation report for his high school ELD class, Stephen Hochschild began by asking his students to brainstorm a list of activities, events, and places they associated with their culture. For example, Karina Diaz wrote *play soccer, dance to Mexican music, Navidad, 10 de Mayo, Mexican food, Año Nuevo, my Quinceañera.* Next, he asked them to select a topic to write about and to draw a picture of themselves, recreating the scene. Diaz drew a picture of herself in a yellow dress, wearing a tiara, standing by her cake, surrounded by friends. Next, he asked them to create a storyboard to capture the sequence of events. Each event was placed on a separate white square and included a picture and a description. Hochschild urged the students to use sequence words like *first, next,* and *then,* and to reorder the squares multiple times to create the order that would best convey the information, before gluing the squares onto colored paper. Their storyboards then became their road map for composing. Figure 4.7 shows Karina Diaz's saturation report on her Quinceañera.

USING PROJECT-BASED LEARNING TO TEACH
21ST-CENTURY SKILLS AND INFORMATIONAL TEXT STRUCTURES

Media skills and research purposefully were blended into the CCSS as a whole because in order to be ready for college, workforce training, and life in a technological society, "students need the ability to gather, comprehend, evaluate, synthesize, and report on information and ideas, to conduct original research in order to answer questions or solve problems, and to analyze and create a high volume and extensive range of print and non-print texts in media forms old and new" (National Governors Association, 2010, p. 4). One way to help students develop 21st-century skills and meet the CCSS is through project-based learning (PBL). PBL is an inquiry-based approach to learning that is teacher facilitated but student driven. Most PBL is focused on a "driving" or essential question that involves solving a problem arising in everyday life. PBL projects are intended to teach significant standards-based content; designed to integrate critical thinking, problem solving, collaboration, and communication; focused on an inquiry that involves creating something new; organized around an open-ended driving question;

Figure 4.7. Karina Diaz's Saturation Report

My Quinceañera

Everything started when I was dancing with my dad and it was an emotional party. September 19 was my Quinceañera and I was very exited and happy.

In the morning I'm going to do my hair. My hair is very pretty. I look at my self in the mirror and I think final it is my Quinceañera. The hair dresser sprays my hair and I smell sweet perfume like summer.

Then we went to my home and then I puted on my new and beautiful dress. My beautiful dress is yellow strap less and very elegant. It is tight on top and very wide on the bottom like a dilicieos banana cake. My dad looks at me and seias "Te miras muy diferente y bonita y te quiero mucho." You look very diferent and pretty and I love you very much. I feel very emotional and happy.

We go to church in a big black hummer. My whole family was in the car. Wen I sied the big brown church I'm so nervous and my hands are shaking. I sed my pardino in the front of the church at the altar. He sed the mass in a loud voize. There are white candles around me. I also see yellos sun flowers and everyone looking at me.

Then we go to the party. We eat "barbacoa" met it is spicy weth red chili salsa. It meks me think about my granma's cooking in Guadalajara. We finish eating and it is time for the dance. I started dancing with my dad and I was very excited. The music is slow and gentle. He seid you are not a little girl you are a like a woman now. I feel warm. I am so prud to be a woman now.

Source: Karina Diaz, 2014. Reprinted with permission.

geared toward an end product, including a presentation that generates a genuine need to know; and presented to an audience beyond classmates and the teacher (Larmer & Mergendoller, 2012). Because PBL is process as well as product oriented, opportunities for revision and reflection also are woven into the curriculum.

THE DESIGN YOUR PERFECT SCIENCE CLASSROOM ACTIVITY

In her 7th-grade English language arts classroom, Lisa Tarkoff resolved to put PBL into practice and to use it to reinforce the informational text structures she had been teaching her students. Through serendipity, a community member had just made a generous donation to be used for school improvement. Tarkoff immediately resolved to enlist students in designing a "dream" science lab that would lead to the actual remodeling of the science classroom. The Design Your Perfect Science Classroom task she presented to her students is shown in Figure 4.8.

Tarkoff's first step was to form design teams, with group members assuming the following roles: project manager, secretary, mathematician, finance manager, visual artist, construction manager, and product/market researcher. Teams adopted names

Figure 4.8. Design the Perfect Science Classroom

Task: Working as a member of a design team, you are assigned to design and build the perfect science classroom. You are competing against other teams to "win the contract" of influencing the design of the science lab. Your audience is the school principal, the science teacher, and school board. The classroom is just an empty room, and you are to fill it with furniture, technology, and science equipment. The project must include the following elements (see grading rubric):

1. Scale floor plan of the room and objects within it
2. Perspective drawing illustrating the room in 3-D
3. 3-D model
4. An inventory which outlines where the items are purchased and how much they cost
5. A written proposal
6. Design file
7. Presentation

Source: Lisa Tarkoff, 2014. Reprinted with permission.

such as the Fast Fix-IT Crew and created a design logo. In Tarkoff's school, ELs are mainstreamed into the regular language arts classes. The collaborative nature of this Design Your Perfect Science Classroom project enabled those students to play an active role on the design team according to their strengths. For example, those with less language proficiency but with mathematical or artistic skills could contribute by creating budgets or scale drawings. Additionally, all of the writing tasks were done independently and received the teacher's feedback.

Stage 1 of the project was "reconnaissance." Tarkoff's students were dispatched to the science lab as researchers to observe the classroom in action. Taking on the role of critics and silent observers, they took notes on the outdated equipment, the graffiti on the desktops, the not-so-smart whiteboard, and so on, and made lists of what they felt needed to be improved. This led to the first writing task—a *description* of the current science classroom with sufficient concrete detail that a reader could picture it clearly.

Stage 2 of the project involved research into the question, "What is an ideal science lab?" Students consulted websites such as www.creativelearningsystems.com and schoolsofthought.blogs.cnn.com, and read articles about SmartLabs, including "My View: What a 21st-Century Science Classroom Should Look Like" by Tim Magner, former executive director of the Partnership for 21st Century Skills. This led to the second informational writing task, a *comparison/contrast* of the ideal science classroom and the existing classroom at the school. After watching a YouTube video on how to create a Google Form Survey, students designed and launched Stage 3 of the project, a question survey about what teachers and students liked about the current science classroom and what they thought the new science lab should include. During Stage 4 of the project, students returned to measure the science classroom and to draw the basic outline of the structure. Subsequently, they received guidance on how to develop a 2-dimensional scale floor plan, followed by a 3-dimensional model of the room, to scale. Students constructed these models out of cardboard or tag board, with cut-out openings for windows and doors, and foam core or plastic for furniture and storage units. Figure 4.9 shows a visual of a 3-dimensional model of the science classroom. In Stage 5, students learned to keep track of expenses using a Google Spreadsheet, and included items needed, quantity, unit price, total price, labor costs, and vendor or supplier.

Having researched their ideal science classroom, students were ready to develop a written proposal in Stage 6 of the project.

Figure 4.9. 3-D Model of a Science Classroom

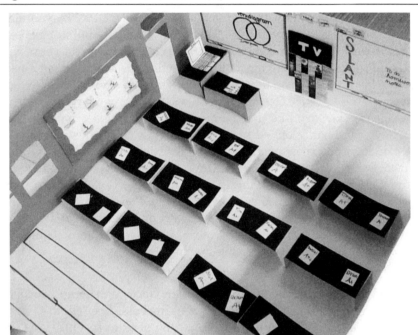

Source: Lisa Tarkoff, 2014. Reprinted with permission.

Students worked independently to create a statement of the *problem* and then propose a *solution*. They received instruction in how to approach their audience (the school principal, science teacher, the school board, and a retired engineer from the community) in a business-like, professional tone and to present their visions for teaching and learning in the new science lab, defend their building design decisions, delineate a *sequence* of steps that must be taken in a specific order to accomplish the renovation, and include their 2- and 3-D scale models and cost estimates. Figure 4.10 presents an Executive Summary by Christine Tran, an EL in Tarkoff's classroom. Subsequently, students met in their design teams to integrate the best aspects of the individual proposals into one team document.

The final stage of the project was to deliver a 10-minute team presentation to the prospective "client" (principal, science teacher, school board, and engineer) using Keynote/Apple TV or another appropriate audiovisual aid to highlight the strengths of the proposal. On the day of the presentation, students rehearsed beforehand and

Figure 4.10. Executive Summary

Students and teachers want to remodel the science lab. Why you may ask well I'm gonna tell you why. The middle school building has been here since the 80's. One of our teachers has been here for 11 years and she said that it hasn't changed at all. Our reasons that we need a new science lab is that we can have a better learning environment. We want to remodel the science classroom because students can have careers in the science category like marine biology, doctors, math, etc. Also we can have more hands on learning, technology, with the new science lab we can do more experiments, and lastly better equipment. My groups remodel and proposal can be ideal for the science room because the paint that we choice can bring in more light into the classroom than regular brown paint. Also we have new desk because honestly who would sit on a desk with gum underneath or writing on it I know I wouldn't. Hopefully this proposal helped you to learn more about why we are remodeling the science classroom.

Source: Christina Tran, 2014. Reprinted with permission.

coached one another on projecting their voices. Although natural leaders arose, every student had a speaking role. The "clients" were very impressed with the professional tone of the presentations. In fact, the engineer favorably compared the written proposals with written proposals he saw in his working career. Tarkoff commented, "The PBL project gave me an opportunity to teach a lot of informational text structures for an authentic purpose. What started off as a simple scale model math project evolved into something with a life of its own and my classroom was transformed. My students became active, enthusiastic learners who were motivated to develop writing and 21st-century skills that will aid them in their future careers."

To Sum Up

- According to the CCSS, informative/explanatory texts "examine and convey complex ideas and information clearly and accurately" in order to inform or teach their readers about a given topic through the "effective selection, organization, and analysis of content."

- Students' success in schooling, the workplace, and society depends on their ability to read informational text and write about it.

- Informative/explanatory writing also leads to substantial opportunities to increase home–school–community connections.

- Proficiency in writing informative/explanatory texts, especially for ELs, often requires instruction in the language resources needed to write informational text, especially when such text includes disciplinary language and content.

- ELs also benefit from in-depth instruction in the organizational features of informational text such as text structures, sequencing, and so forth.

- ELs can develop the sophisticated, abstract language necessary to give readers an accurate, objective, complete, and concise view of a piece of writing through explicit instruction in and practice with writing informative/explanatory texts.

CHAPTER 5

Argumentative Writing and CCSS

As George Hillocks (2011) points out, argumentative writing is the core of critical thinking. In his words, "Argument is not simply a dispute, as when people disagree with one another or yell at each other. Argument is about making a case in support of a claim in everyday affairs—in science, in policy making, in courtrooms, and so forth" (p. 1). Argument writing is essential for success in institutes of higher education as well as professional environments (see Fulkerson, 1996). It is important in all content areas of secondary education. When discussing its use in school contexts, the CCSS explain:

> English language arts students make claims about the worth or meaning of a literary work or works. They defend their interpretations or judgments with evidence from the text(s) they are writing about. In history/social studies, students analyze evidence from multiple primary and secondary sources to advance a claim that is best supported by the evidence, and they argue for a historically or empirically situated interpretation. In science, students make claims in the form of statements or conclusions that answer questions or address problems. (Appendix A, p. 23)

Despite its importance, most students find argumentative writing challenging (Salahu-Din, Persky, & Miller, 2008). Perie, Grigg, and Donahue (2005), for instance, found in their study that only 15% of the 12th-grade students who scored proficient in writing could write essays containing a clear arguable claim and consistent supportive evidence. A number of other researchers (Biancarosa & Snow, 2004; Graham & Perin, 2007; Langer, 2002) have also noted the difficulties learners have mastering the advanced reading skills, which entail synthesizing multiple texts with similar and competing perspectives, necessary for critical literacy and argumentative, evidence-based writing. Chambliss and Murphy (2002) have explored the problems that students encounter learning particular argumentative structures. Other researchers have shown additional difficulties learners face, for instance, in generating and critiquing evidence (see, e.g., McCann, 1989), in developing warrants that explain why or how their evidence supports their claims and the underlying assumptions that connect the evidence to their claims (Persky, Daane, & Jin, 2003), and in shaping their writing to their purposes and audiences (Kuhn, 2005). Recognizing these challenges, the CCSS for grades 6–12 call on students to "support claims in an analysis of substantive topics or texts using valid reasoning and relevant and sufficient evidence" (National Governors Association, 2010, p. 41). The standards require students to learn a range of argument structures within multiple disciplines, including history, science, and English language arts.

When composing argumentative texts, writers not only give factual information but also present a reasoned opinion with supporting ideas, and often acknowledge opposing ones. They demonstrate that "their positions, beliefs, and conclusions are valid" (National Governors Association, 2010, Appendix A, p. 23). They write persuasive letters, policy pieces, advertisements, newspaper editorials, opinion articles, and essays. Their purpose is to persuade readers to take specific actions or accept or change viewpoints. This can involve altering readers' beliefs, for example, persuading them to accept new perspectives, take particular actions, or adopt new behavior. They organize their writing in specific ways, evaluate their own arguments critically before making them, discern conflicting perspectives, and methodically respond to opposing views (Ferretti & Lewis, 2013). When writing effective argumentative texts, writers thoroughly understand their topics and support their claims with facts, data sources, statistics, expert testimonials, quotations, and examples. They embrace a professional, authoritative tone. Often, they investigate both sides of an issue and present counterviews when appropriate and then refute those ideas in an effort to persuade their readers to accept their arguments. They use short sentences to emphasize key points, and long and complex sentences to slow readers down and make them reflect on their claims and evidence. To encourage their audience to take particular positions, they use pronouns (like inclusive *we*) and modal auxiliaries (like *should*). Their vocabulary varies greatly, but often includes specific and exact words that prevent ambiguity (*certainly, truly, definitely*), and fixed expressions that are associated with argumentative writing such as *Opponents of this idea claim/maintain that . . .*

Even English learners with moderate to strong levels of English proficiency face particular challenges when learning argumentative writing. Many have not been asked to compose novel arguments before. Those with an emerging level of English proficiency will need instructional support to learn how to announce their topics and engage their readers, write strong thesis statements, link paragraphs and support with smooth transitions to make their writing cohesive, and use academic language. They are in the process of learning the language to incorporate source material effectively and use textual citations to support their interpretations of evidence. Their experiences, backgrounds, and previous practices may not have prepared them to follow the genre- and disciplinary-specific conventions of argumentative writing or understand the values and beliefs associated with these conventions. As Bunch, Kibler, and Pimentel (2012) explain, the argument is "grounded in particular socially and culturally developed values and practices that may or may not align with those of students from different backgrounds" (p. 10). As a result, students may not recognize relevant information required to support their perspective, acknowledge or rebut viewpoints inconsistent with their own, or consider the merits of other views. Their arguments may seem poorly developed, insensitive to pertinent opposing ideas, or unsubstantiated, with inadequate supporting ideas and examples. They are still learning how to evaluate the effectiveness of their evidence and may not have much practice developing their own thesis statements. In some ELs' home countries, China, for instance, students practice argumentative writing extensively for a series of exams that call on them to address a specified thesis statement and are not expected to develop thesis statements independently (Kirkpatrick & Zang, 2011).

Sometimes, EL writing may seem to jump from one point to the next, leading some teachers to erroneously believe that their students are not logical. However, there is nothing illogical about the students. They are just in the process of developing transition words and learning to use them to link sections of their arguments (Lorenz, 1999). They may have received inadequate instruction in argumentative writing and may not understand their audience's knowledge of their topic or ways to establish credibility with particular readers. Studies have shown that their arguments may be significantly shorter and less developed than those of their English-proficient peers (Cumming, 2001). Not having enough to say may be related to the challenges ELs face when asked to write about complex texts that they do not adequately understand (Fillmore &

Fillmore, 2012). For example, when attempting to trace Winston Churchill's argument in his "Blood, Toil, Tears and Sweat" address to Parliament and evaluate his conclusions and opinions, they may have difficulty distinguishing which claims are supported by facts, reasons, and evidence, and which are not (CCSS, Appendix B). Hence they benefit from instruction that leverages and extends their prior content and linguistic knowledge (see Council of Chief State School Officers, 2012; Echevarría et al., 2012; Valdés, Kibler, & Walqui, 2014).Challenges for students at the emergent level include learning to make sense of the academic readings pertaining to argumentative writing assignments. They have difficulty framing, structuring, evaluating, and presenting arguments. They are just beginning to develop the elements of well-formed arguments and the structures of different types of arguments and need much instruction in these areas. They do not know that in arguments, words such as nouns and verbs perform functions that differ from those of their usual functions (e.g., the verb *find* can be turned into a noun *finding*) and that some words can be multiple parts of speech, having the same form whether they are nouns, verbs, or adjectives (e.g., *double, light,* and *wrong*). They are challenged to produce complex clauses or incorporate quotations, as they are in the process of acquiring basic word order. They may have learned the basic function of pronouns to refer to nouns, but they have not learned how to use them to present evidence coherently. Vocabulary is a major hurdle for these students, since they are just learning how to use words to enable "the abstraction, technicality, and development of arguments that characterize advanced literacy tasks" (Schleppegrell, 2004, p. 72).

TYPES OF ARGUMENTS

Argumentative writing generally focuses on either a call to action or a claim. It can be organized into various broad approaches. The first is *opinion writing*, which provides anecdotal, personal opinion as evidence for claims. The second is *fact-based* or *evidence-based writing*, which provides factual evidence, usually from text, to support claims. Many types of writing, including *persuasive writing* and *literary analyses*, can be either opinion-based or fact-based.

Argumentative writing also can be organized in terms of whether it presents an Aristotelian, adversarial approach or a Rogerian, consensus-building approach. *Toulmin arguments*, espoused by philosopher Stephen Toulmin, support the Aristotelian approach. They provide evidence for a claim and address readers' concerns. *Rogerian arguments*, named after the psychologist Carl Rogers, compare options to a problem or course of action, examining their relative importance. In this type of argument, the writer avoids emotionally sensitive language and phrases language in as neutral a way as possible to prevent alienating readers.

One other way of looking at argument writing is described by Hillocks (2011). Drawing on Aristotle, he divides arguments into three kinds: fact (using previous knowledge to derive claims, warrants, and evidence); judgment (defending and evaluating warrants explicitly); and policy (entailing not only explicit reference to the reasoning underlying warrants and claims but also a definite course of action readers should take, e.g., adopted for the sake of expediency, facility, or to address a problem). He argues that these three types should be presented sequentially, since they build in complexity.

Common types of argumentative writing include: expository writing, persuasive writing, analytical essays, rhetorical analysis, research papers, and personal essays. *Expository writing*, which also may include informative writing, focuses on the writers' "explanation" of issues, themes, and ideas. It is included in argumentative writing because it often states claims and provides supporting evidence. In *persuasive writing*, writers call on their readers to take a specific action. In the *analytical essay*, which includes literary analyses, writers analyze, examine, and interpret events, books, poems, or other types of textual evidence to support a claim. *Rhetorical analysis,* a type of analytical essay, describes the way authors compose and organize their texts to support their claims. When writing *research papers*, students use external sources to support claims, often citing about the same number of references per claim made. When writing *personal essays* (such as blogs, diary entries, opinion pieces), students make a compelling case to support a claim that is based on their opinion and subjective reasoning.

ELEMENTS OF TEXT-BASED ARGUMENTATIVE WRITING

The CCSS place a premium on developing students' ability to "read closely to determine what the text says explicitly and to make logical inferences from it," as well as to support one's claims and conclusions drawn from the text by citing specific textual evidence (p. 5). Whether students are writing about literature or nonfiction, and whether they are developing an interpretive claim or presenting an evaluative argument, most text-based analytical essays have certain common elements, which students need to practice in order to become proficient. As was mentioned in Chapter 1, many teachers of ELs avoid teaching their students to write text-based argumentative essays because they think the skills required are too sophisticated for the population they serve. Yet, the architects of the CCSS strongly believe that all students should be held to the same high expectations, including students who are ELs.

Let's look at some activities to help ELs write text-based analytical essays.

Using the HoT S-C Team Activity to Write an Introduction

One constraint EL students face when they are writing to teacher-directed prompts is how to begin. HoT S-C Team (*Hook/TAG/Story-Conflict/Thesis*) is a strategy that can help students plan what to include in an introduction to a text-based essay and how to organize that information. The student must first consider how to open his or her essay in a way that gets the reader's attention. Using a hook, such as a quotation from the text, a thought-provoking question, dialogue, or a statement to make people think, can capture the reader's interest. For example, here are some hooks written as a model by the teacher for an interpretive essay that a group of middle school ELs were asked to write about why the children treated Margot so cruelly in Ray Bradbury's "All Summer in a Day" (1998).

> *Quotation:* "And then, of course, the biggest crime of all was that she had come here only five years ago from earth, and she remembered the sun and the way the sun was and the sky was when she was four years old in Ohio."

> *Description/Figurative Language*: Like a pack of wolves, the children pounced upon Margot and viciously attacked her, shoving her in the closet.

> *Question*: What could have motivated a group of 9-year-olds to turn upon one of their classmates and treat her so cruelly?

> *A Statement to Make People Think*: Peer pressure often can influence children to behave badly, especially if there is a bully in the group.

The next step in writing the introduction is to identify the title, author, and genre (TAG) of the text. TAG sentences often start with a prepositional phrase:

In (type of genre and name of text) by (author), (x happens).

As mentioned previously, ELs often have difficulty with this structure and have a tendency to write: *In "All Summer in a Day" by Ray Bradbury is about* . . . . One option is to have students word the TAG sentence without a preposition by starting with the author's name: *Ray Bradbury's short story, "All Summer in a Day," deals with a young girl named Margot who is persecuted because she has knowledge of the sun that her classmates do not have.*

As part of the TAG or right after the TAG, the student should include a brief statement that summarizes the text and should provide background information, including the issue, problem, or conflict it addresses. This statement often will lead into the writer's thesis. A thesis statement in an essay is the claim the writer makes in response to the prompt. Using the analogy "the thesis statement is the key that drives your essay" helps students to understand the important role the thesis or claim plays in focusing the argument that is to follow. It is also useful to demonstrate what a thesis is not as well as what it is, as in the distinction below.

A thesis statement is not just an explanation of what your essay will be about.

> *Example:* This essay will be about why the children behaved cruelly toward Margot. (Not a thesis statement)

A thesis statement advances your interpretation of the topic or issue you are discussing.

> *Example:* The children behave cruelly toward Margot because they sense that she is different and so they ostracize her.

Giving ELs the components of an introduction (as in the example below) cut up and inserted into envelopes, and having them work in groups to put them in order can help them to internalize the structure of an introduction.

1. Motivated by jealousy and succumbing to peer pressure, they cruelly lock Margot in the closet, depriving her of her long-awaited moment in the sun.

2. "And then of course, the biggest crime of all was that she had come here from Earth, and she remembered the sun and the way the sun was and the sky was when she was four years old."

3. In the story "All Summer in a Day" by Ray Bradbury, the children of the planet Venus, where it rains for 7 years with no hint of sunshine, treat Margot like a criminal because she has knowledge about the sun that they don't possess. (Note: The correct order is 2, 3, 1.)

While some teachers might see the HoT S-C Team approach in Figure 5.1 as somewhat formulaic, ELs need to be exposed to form making, in order to lower the textual constraints of essay writing, before they can engage in form breaking (Norris & Ortega, 2000). In other words, students must be adept at replicating text structures before they can make informed decisions about how to manipulate the structure of their compositions and even choose to violate certain writing conventions—such as selectively inserting sentence fragments into their prose for effect.

USING QUOTATIONS AND COMMENTARY
TO SUPPORT A TEXT-BASED ARGUMENT

The CCSS note that in order to be college and career ready, "students must grapple with works of exceptional craft and thought whose range extends across genres, cultures, and centuries" (p. 5). As students analyze and make inferences about these complex texts and present a claim about the meaning of these works, they will be called upon to support their interpretations or evaluations with textual evidence throughout the body of their essay. ELs, who may have had little practice composing text-based analytical essays, may not be familiar with the rules for quoting from the text as well as for embedding quotations in their own sentences and commenting on the significance of these quotations. The following are three rules that may help ELs embed quotations in their essays:

1. Introduce the quotation using a signal phrase such as *The author states, maintains, remarks, writes,* and so forth. Figure 5.2 includes a table of useful verbs that students can use to introduce quotations. These verbs often are called reporting verbs. It is important to point out that the verbs are not all interchangeable. Before selecting a verb,

it is important that students understand that verbs vary in terms of their strength and the extent to which they can objectively describe the writer's intentions. For example, verbs such as *argue, contend,* and *maintain* are stronger verbs than *indicate* and *suggest.* Students also need to consider the grammatical restrictions of the verbs they choose. For example, the verb *mention* is especially difficult for ELs to use because they frequently confuse the verb *mention* with *think* and end up writing, "mention about + something."

2. Present the quotation using proper punctuation, as in the following example from an essay analyzing theme in the magazine article "The Man in the Water," by Roger Rosenblatt (1982), about the crash of Air Florida Flight 90 and a man who sacrificed his life to save others from the disaster. Rosenblatt remarks, "If the man in the water gave a lifeline to the people gasping for survival, he likewise gave a lifeline to those who observed him."

   Note: This would be a good opportunity to point out some punctuation rules to ELs, such as commas after introductory phrases, capitalization of the "I" in the first word of the quotation, and final periods going inside the quotation marks.

3. Follow up the quotation with a sentence that explains or comments on it. Effective phrases to begin commentary with are *This suggests that . . .* ; *In other words, the author is implying that . . .* ; *These words communicate that . . .* ; *This quotation shows that . . .* ; *This is significant because . . .* ; *This reminds us to . . .* ; *In essence, the author is saying that . . .* ; and so forth.

Figure 5.1. HoT S-C Team

How Do I Begin?

The Introduction to Your Interpretive Essay

4 Parts: HoT S-C T

(**Ho**T **S-C** Team) = (**H**ook/**T**AG/**S**tory-**C**onflict/**T**hesis)

Hook: Begin your introductory paragraph with an attention grabber or "hook" to capture the reader's interest. It might include *one* of the following:

- Opening with an exciting moment from the story

Figure 5.1. HoT S-C Team (continued)

- An interesting description
- Dialogue
- Quotation from the text
- A statement to make people think
- An anecdote (a brief story)
- A thought-provoking question (a question that makes people think)

1. TAG: Follow the "hook" with a TAG (title/author/genre = type of literature such as short story, narrative, novel, play, poem) that identifies all three parts of TAG for the reader.

2. Summary Statement-Conflict: As a part of the TAG, or right after the TAG, include a brief summary of the story and its conflict. Usually two or three sentences are enough to give background information to the reader about the story and the conflict.

3. Thesis Statement: The thesis statement in an essay is the claim the writer makes in response to the prompt. The thesis statement is the "key" that will "drive" your essay. Do people go on a trip with no idea of where to go? No, they look at a map or check the Internet for driving directions. Your job as a writer is to "map" your essay for the readers. Tell the readers where you will take them.

Source: Olson, Scarcella, and Matuchniak, 2013. Reprinted with permission.

One strategy to help students practice developing commentary is to provide them with a sentence that includes a quotation and to ask them to generate a commentary sentence to follow the quotation. For example, Roger Rosenblatt's observation about the man in the water might elicit the following commentary:

> Rosenblatt remarks, "If the man in the water gave a lifeline to the people gasping for survival, he likewise gave a lifeline to those who observed him." In other words, Rosenblatt is suggesting that to observe such an act of selflessness and heroism gives us hope and inspiration.

It is also helpful to engage students in elaboration by having them comment on their comments:

> Rosenblatt remarks, "If the man in the water gave a lifeline to the people gasping for survival, he likewise gave a lifeline to those who observed him." In other words, Rosenblatt is suggesting that to observe such an act of selflessness and heroism gives

Figure 5.2. Reporting Verbs

Below is a chart containing useful verbs that students can use to introduce quotations or report on authors' ideas. These verbs often are called reporting verbs. Please note that the verbs are not all interchangeable. Before selecting a verb, it is important that students understand the meaning of the verb and its grammatical restrictions.

acknowledge	add	affirm
argue	assert	believe
challenge the view that	claim	conclude
consider	contend	deny
describe	discuss	emphasize
examine	explain	hypothesize
imply	indicate	insist
maintain	mention	negate
note	point out	posit the view
propose	question	raise the question
recommend	refute	reject
remark	say	show
speculate	state	suggest
support the view	suspect	take the perspective
theorize	think	view
wonder		

us hope and inspiration. He teaches us that ordinary people are capable of extraordinary acts of courage.

Acknowledging and Refuting Counterarguments

The CCSS Writing Standards for argument call upon students to:

1. Introduce precise claim(s), distinguish the claim(s) from alternate or opposing claims and create an organization that establishes clear relationships among claim(s), counterclaims, reasons, and evidence.

2. Develop claim(s) and counterclaims fairly, supplying evidence for each while pointing out the strengths and limitations of both in a manner that anticipates the audience's knowledge level and concerns.
3. Use words, phrases, and clauses to link the major sections of the text, create cohesion, and clarify the relationships between claim(s) and reasons, between reasons and evidence, and between claim(s) and counterclaims. (National Governors Association, 2010, p. 45)

For ELs who have had little experience writing argumentative essays, let alone acknowledging and refuting counterarguments, it is helpful to scaffold instruction by beginning with a more accessible text type, the persuasive letter, and to have students write about real-world issues they want to persuade a familiar audience to agree to or with rather than to have them immediately write about complex texts. This will enable them to practice anticipating objections that an audience might have to their argument and overcoming those objections with logical reasons or alternatives.

Students can be given the following prompt for this activity.

Writing Prompt: The Persuasive Letter

Choose one thing that you would like to persuade someone to do. Write a letter to persuade your chosen audience. Your letter should show that you have done the following:

> Clearly stated what you want and why
> Used a tone suited to your audience
> Predicted two possible objections your audience might have
> Met those objections with logical arguments
> Followed the standard letter form of greeting, body, and closing

(Bergquist, in Olson, 1992)

After students have brainstormed who their audience is (mom, a classmate, their soccer coach, the owner of a local store, etc.), they can first practice orally by dividing into pairs and role-playing the parts of persuader and audience, with the audience coming up with objections to the persuader's request, and the persuader coming up with arguments to overcome those objections. For example:

Persuader: Mom, will you let me take three friends to Farrell's ice cream parlor for my birthday?
Audience: No, Farrell's is too expensive.
Persuader: I'll help pay with my allowance.

Once they have practiced orally, students can participate in a silent exchange activity where, as partners, they pass notes back and forth in the roles of persuader and audience. These notes can then be used as prewriting for their persuasive letters.

The Persuasive Letter activity can serve as a bridge to the argumentative essay. For instance, students could be given the following prompt about the nonfiction article "Steve Irwin: Wild by Nature," that describes events leading up to his death from a stingray barb and the aftermath (Wulff, 2006).

Writing Prompt: Steve Irwin: Heroic or Foolhardy?

In the *People* magazine article "Steve Irwin: Wild by Nature (Wulff, 2006), the author portrays Steve Irwin as a "wildlife warrior" who has left an important legacy of wildlife conservation to his wife, Terri, and daughter, Bindi. Yet, she acknowledges that while he is beloved by many, others perceive him as reckless and foolhardy, someone who not only tempted fate but who put the lives of others in danger as well. Where do you stand? Do you perceive him as heroic or foolhardy, noble or crass, altruistic or in it for the money and fame? Was his death tragic or inevitable? Write an argumentative essay clearly stating your position about Steve Irwin, his cause, and his actions. Support your opinion with facts, reasons, details, and/or examples. Address the concerns of those who may not agree with you. Convince them that your point of view is best.

When acknowledging and refuting a counterargument, ELs may benefit from the sentence frames in Figure 5.3.

COLOR-CODING FOR REVISION

English learners who have been in English language development programs that focus primarily on literal comprehension often tend to rely on retelling when writing a text-based analytical essay, as a way to prove that they understood what they read, rather than offering interpretation and commentary to support their argument. As Bereiter and Scardamalia (1987) point out, novice, inexperienced, and struggling writers use a simplified version of the idea-generation

Figure 5.3. Sentence Frames for Acknowledging and Refuting Counterarguments

Some people may argue that _____. However, _____.

Although one could argue that _____, another, more compelling perspective is that _____.

While it is true that _____, it does not necessarily follow that _____.

While some might perceive _____, what they fail to consider is that _____.

Admittedly, _____.

Nevertheless, _____.

process that they call *knowledge-telling*, which consists of retrieving information from long-term memory and converting the writing task into simply regurgitating what is known about a topic. More expert writers, on the other hand, engage in a complex composing process known as *knowledge-transformation*, in which they analyze the writing task and plan what to say and how to say it in accordance with rhetorical, communicative, and pragmatic constraints. One way to help students move from knowledge-telling to knowledge-transformation is to help them make their thinking visible, using a color-coding process, after they have composed a first draft of an essay.

Teachers first designate three colors for the types of assertions that constitute a text-based analytical essay and say the following:

> Plot summary reiterates what is obvious and known in a text. Reiterate means to repeat in order to make something very clear. Plot summary is *yellow* because it's like the sun. It makes things as plain as day. We need some plot summary to orient our reader to the facts, but we don't need to retell the entire story. Commentary is *blue* like the ocean because the writer goes beneath the surface of things to look at the deeper meaning and to offer opinions, interpretations, insights, and "Aha's." Supporting detail is *green* because, like the color, it brings together the facts of the text (yellow) with your interpretation of it (blue). It is what glues together plot summary and commentary. It's your evidence to support your claims, including quotations from the text.

The next step is to model the process by color-coding a sample paragraph about *For One Quake Survivor, Self-Help in the Face of Seeming Helplessness* by Mark Magnier (2011), written one week after the Japanese earthquake and tsunami (see Figure 5.4).

Figure 5.4. Color-Coding for Revision

(green)	"As the death toll keeps rising, most of what we hear from Japan is bad news.
(green)	But within all the sadness are these few stories of triumph and downright determination."
(yellow)	One such story recounted in the article "For One Quake Survivor, Self-Help in the Face of Seeming Helplessness," by *LA Times* journalist Mark Magnier, describes how one man risked his life to save family members from the devastating tsunami in Ishinomaki, Japan.
(yellow)	Donning scuba gear, Akaiwa plunged into a violent torrent and dodged floating cars and battered houses in order to locate his missing wife and bring her to safety.
(blue)	When disaster strikes, it often motivates ordinary people to perform extraordinary acts of courage.
(blue)	This is especially significant because it renews our hope in the power that each of us has to find the hero within us and to make a difference.

After students are introduced to the color-coding system, they can practice coding sample essays on the same topic that are marginal/not pass (1–3 on a 6-point scale) and adequate to strong pass (4–6 on a 6-point scale). Starting with the weaker paper, students will notice that most of the sentences fall into the yellow category, whereas the stronger paper has a balance of yellow, green, and blue. Students can then apply the color-coding strategy to their own first drafts to visibly see whether they have simply summarized or whether they have provided ample textual evidence and commentary. The coded draft then becomes a visible guide for revision.

IMAGE GRAMMAR

The CCSS Anchor Standards for Language note that students "must come to appreciate that language is at least as much a matter of craft as of rules and be able to choose words, syntax, and punctuation to express themselves and achieve particular functions and rhetorical effects" (p. 51). Crafting sentences for rhetorical effects is a special challenge for ELs, especially when writing analytical essays, because they are in the process of learning their audience's expectations and developing the linguistic resources to meet them. One strategy to help students with sentence variety is to teach them image grammar brush strokes. According to Harry Noden (2011), "The writer is an artist, painting images of life and specific and identifiable brush strokes, images as realistic as Wyeth and as abstract as Picasso. In the act of creation, the writer, like the artist, relies on fundamental elements" (p. 1). He continues, "To paint images . . . requires an understanding of image grammar—a rhetoric of writing techniques that provides writers with artistic grammatical options" (p. 2).

Five specific brush strokes can help ELs enhance their writer's craft through words, syntax, and punctuation. Training in the brush strokes works best if the teacher introduces each brush stroke, models it, provides students with multiple opportunities to practice, and then requires them to add a brush stroke to an essay they are revising. The examples below were used to help students revise an essay on Mark Magnier's message in *For One Quake Survivor, Self-Help in the Face of Seeming Helplessness* (2011). For each example, the teacher presented a visual of the Japanese tsunami, including actual video footage, and then left the model sentence up as students generated a brush stroke about Magnier's article. The brush strokes are presented in order of difficulty.

Painting with Action Verbs

Action verbs or strong verbs transform still photos into motion pictures by helping the reader to visualize the action. Writers can energize their sentences by using active rather than passive voice (e.g., The tsunami *hit* the town—active—instead of The town *was hit* by the tsunami—passive), that is, by avoiding the use of being verbs (is, are, was, were, be, being, been).

> ***Teacher Model:*** On March 11, 2011, the Tohuku earthquake *struck* violently, setting off a tsunami that *raced* into shore, *swept* up boats and cars, *hurled* them into buildings, and *wreaked* havoc through the country.

> ***Student Sample:*** When Hideaki arrived to Ishinomaki, he *raced* and put on his scuba gear, *jumped* into the raging tsunami waters, and *battled* against the tsunami wave.

Painting with Adjectives Out of Order

Adjectives out of order are adjectives set off with a comma that follow rather than precede the noun they describe.

Teacher Model: The Japanese tsunami survivors, *shocked* and *devastated,* prayed for their lost loved ones.

Student Sample: Hideaki Akaiwa, *worried* and *restless*, did not wait for help and took the matter into his own hand.

Painting with Appositives

An appositive is a noun or noun phrase set off by commas that follows/describes the noun it identifies.

Teacher Model: The tsunami, *a huge and ravenous wave,* attacked the shore, swallowing up whole buildings in one gulp.

Student Sample: The tsunami, *a giant monster,* was "picking up cars like they were toys and destroying buildings like they were paper."

Painting with Participles

A participle is an *ing* verb (or a series of *ing* verbs) tagged on to the beginning or end of a sentence. A participial phrase is the *ing* verb plus its modifiers and complements.

Teacher Model: Roaring in from the sea, crashing into the shore, crushing cars as if they were toys, the tsunami engulfed Japan.

Student Sample: Praying they would both make it out safely, Hideaki gave his wife a respirator to swim underwater.

Painting with Absolutes

An absolute phrase typically consists of a noun and a participial adjective. The adjective often consists of a verb form ending in *-ing*.

Teacher Model: Hearts pumping, adrenaline racing the frightened people ran from the deadly wave in a desperate effort to save their lives.

Student Sample: Fear growing, he swam through the dark and dangerous water which was very scary.

Explicitly teaching ELs the elements of text-based analytical writing and enabling them to practice can make the process of argument writing much less daunting because students will be better equipped with the skills and strategies to plan, draft, and revise. In a large randomized field trial of an academic literacy intervention serving students in grades 6–12 in a district with 88% ELs, students receiving instruction in how to write introductions, embedding quotes and providing commentary, color-coding, and brush strokes, scored significantly higher on a text-based analytical writing assessment than students in the control condition who did not receive this training (Kim et al., 2011; Olson et al., 2012). In addition to demonstrating higher test scores and greater growth in writing at the end of the treatment period, treatment students also had significantly higher percentages of TAGS (title, author, genre), commentary, appositives, and adjectives out of order, and their essays were significantly longer than the essays of their peers in the control condition (Matuchniak, 2013; Matuchniak, Olson, & Scarcella, 2014).

TEACHING THE TOULMIN MODEL OF ARGUMENT USING A CRIME SCENE INVESTIGATION REPORT

To help her 7th-grade students, some of whom were mainstreamed ELs, to meet the CCSS for argument writing, Liz Harrington was interested in teaching them how to use the Toulmin model of argument writing. Fortunately for Harrington, she attended a workshop presented by George Hillocks (2011), who gave her a terrific idea for having students become investigators who, after analyzing a crime scene, were tasked with making a claim about whether or not a certain party to an unfortunate and potentially suspicious event should be taken in for questioning. The students were to base this claim on the evidence, providing warrants that explained how the evidence supported the claim, as well as qualifications or rebuttals or counterarguments that refuted competing claims (p. xix).

She began the lesson by inviting students to share their prior knowledge of television shows and movies they had watched that involve CSI teams investigating crime scenes. Once students had developed some background knowledge, she explained that they would have an opportunity to act as crime scene investigators to determine whether the witness in a case was telling the truth or not. She then provided students with the visual in Figure 5.5 and the written scenario that Hillocks adapted from *Crime and Puzzlement*

Figure 5.5. Slip or Trip?

At five-feet-six and a hundred and ten pounds, Queenie Volupides was a sight to behold and to clasp. When she tore out of the house after a tiff with her husband, Arthur, she went to the country club where there was a party going on.

She left the club shortly before one in the morning and invited a few friends to follow her home and have one more drink. They got to the Volupides' house about ten minutes after Queenie, who met them at the door and said, "Something terrible happened. Arthur slipped and fell on the stairs. He was coming down for another drink—he still had the glass in his hand—and I think he's dead. Oh, my God—what shall I do?"

The autopsy conducted later concluded that Arthur had died from a wound on the head and confirmed that he'd been drunk.

Reprinted with permission of David R. Godine, Publisher, Inc.

2 (Treat, 1982). Cautioning that witnesses are not always reliable, Harrington asked students to form CSI teams and to collect evidence regarding Queenie Volupides's account of her husband's accidental death (or was it a homicide?).

Harrington asked students, after collaborating on their collection of evidence, to make a preliminary *claim* about whether they thought Queenie was a credible witness who could be believed. They were unanimous in declaring that Queenie was lying. However, taking a clue from Hillocks, Harrington noted that the argument they were constructing at this early point in the investigation was an argument of judgment, not of absolute fact, and proposed that they add a *qualifier* to the claim: Queenie is *probably* lying. Smith, Wilhelm, and Fredricksen (2012) note that a good way to substantiate a claim with evidence or data is to answer the question "What makes you say so?" (p. 16). In this case, students noted that although Queenie said Arthur slipped as he was coming down the stairs for another drink, the glass was still in his hand. To move from the evidence to a *warrant*, the next step is to ask, "So what?" or "What allows you to move from those grounds to that claim?" (p. 16). Introducing the terms *as a rule* and *generally*, Harrington guided the students to provide a warrant to support their evidence: For example, *As a rule, when people fall forward with an object in their hand, they drop that object in order to grab on to something to break their fall or to protect themselves from injury.*

Since most of Harrington's students were monolingual English speakers and her ELs were very advanced, she taught them the vocabulary words *prone* (lying face down) and *supine* (lying on one's back face up) to describe the position of Arthur's body. They noted, "The man's body is lying supine at the bottom of the stairs. As a rule, if you fall forward, you would most likely fall face first and the body would be lying prone." She also gave the students sentence stems like *According to the witness . . .* to introduce Queenie's testimony; *One might argue that . . . ; however, . . .* to acknowledge and refute a counterargument; and *After thoroughly examining all the evidence, I have concluded that . . .* to make a final conclusion, followed by a recommendation. Figure 5.6 includes an excerpt from the CSI report written by her student Diego Ramirez.

While Diego is clearly a highly proficient writer, Hillocks had success with ELs with slightly lower levels of English proficiency, as in the following example, which, while less articulate and sophisticated, still indicates a high level of reasoning:

> The last reason I believe she is lying is because the things on the wall are straight. They seem liked they hadn't been disturb. If someone falls down the stairs, they will try to hold on to anything. Especially if you see things in the wall you will try to brake your fall. (p. 30)

Harrington remarked, "I thought that the Toulmin model might be too sophisticated for my students to grasp. But Hillocks' *Slip or Trip?* lesson helped me make the idea of basing one's claims on evidence and backing up that evidence with warrants clear to them. And being crime scene investigators kept them thoroughly engaged. I have seen them use expressions like 'as a rule' and 'one could argue that' in other argument papers."

Figure 5.6. CSI Report

I walked into the scene in Mrs. Volupides' living room shortly after one in the morning and took in the sight of a shocked woman standing over her lifeless husband who was lying at the foot of the stair case. According to the witness, Mrs. Volupides, her husband had fallen down a flight of stairs while coming down for another drink. After hearing this statement I stepped up to examine Mr. Volupides' body.

As I approached his body the first thing I noticed was the he was supine at the foot of the stairs, rather than prone. I thought this to be quite unusual, for when someone falls down a fleet of stairs they usually land prone. One could argue that a person could slip backwards and fall down facing upwards, however, but their head would end up on or facing the stairs and his feet on the steps. Not only did Mr. Volupides land in an unusual position, his hair and clothes were also still neat and in good condition. Generally if you fall your clothes would be untidy and ruffled, rather than staying neat. Another sight that I noticed was that the glass was still in Mr. Volupides' hand. Mr. Volupides would have dropped it as he fell or let go of it to reach for support. Even if he did keep it safe in his hand for a reason such as not wanting it to shatter all over the stairs, as a rule the impact of the fall on his body would have made him drop the glass. It is to my surprise that Mr. Volupides did not let go of the glass to grab onto the railing before his tumble. . . . From this evidence, Mrs. Volupides' statement is starting to seem inaccurate, because there is no sign of disturbance. This evidence supports the fact that Mr. Volupides did not take a tumble down the stairs. Finally, after examining all this evidence, I move on to ponder on the witness's statement.

First I asked Mrs. Volupides to please explain her story. She told me that she had gotten into a bit of a quarrel with her husband, Mr. Volupides, and went to the country club, where there was a party going on. After settling down and having a few drinks with her friends at the country club she decided that she would invite them over for one last drink. Mrs. Volupides had arrived ten minutes before her guests, and it was during this time at home when she discovered Mr. Volupides lying supine at the foot of the stairs. When her friends arrived Mrs. Volupides exclaimed to them what happened. There are certain details in her story that bring on suspicion. If Mrs. Volupides had found her husband lying at the foot of the stairs before her friends arrived, she should have contacted help immediately instead of waiting for her friends to arrive. Generally if one were to discover a sight such as this then they would immediately contact help rather than wait.

Finally after thoroughly examining all this evidence and the witness's statement, I have come to conclude that Mrs. Volupides is not

Figure 5.6. CSI Report (continued)

telling the truth. . . . It is best to now take Mrs. Volupides into further questioning and further examine the crime scene for samples of DNA evidence.

Source: Diego Ramirez, 2014. Reprinted with permission.

SCAFFOLDING INSTRUCTION TO TEACH ARGUMENT: THE SUPERHERO UNIT

Heather Wolpert-Gawron, full-time middle school teacher and author of *Writing Behind Every Door: Teaching Common Core Writing Across the Content Areas* (2014), wanted to start off the school year in her 8th-grade English language arts classroom with a bang. She created an iMovie, *Superman* (Main Title Sequence), showing photographs and animated images set to music by John Williams. At the end of this visual display and rousing score, the iMovie concludes with the following text:

> This school year, you are embarking on an adventure. Are you up for the challenge of a lifetime?
> If you were a superhero, who would you be?
> If you were a superhero, what would you stand for?
> If you were a superhero, what would be your superpower?
> If you were a superhero, what would be your Achilles heel, your weakness?
> If you were a superhero, for whom would you fight?
> Welcome to 8th grade, and the Semester of the Superheroes . . .

Thus began a year-long unit in which students were immersed in the study and creation of superheroes, integrating reading, writing, listening and speaking, science, art, and technology, and culminating in advocacy speeches that students presented, in costume, before a mock United Nations audience.

The unit began with the writing of a narrative and the reading and researching of informational texts. Wolpert-Gawron's assignment was as follows:

> All superheroes came from somewhere. Where they came from and how they became heroes are called origin stories. A great origin story isn't just about writing a fun story. Believable origin stories are seeded with facts. In this case, you will be given

the choice of writing a science fiction story or a historical fiction story. This will take research as well as a thorough knowledge of your character and his or her abilities, foibles, and background.

After teaching minilessons on hooks, plot structure, character traits, and theme, Wolpert-Gawron turned to research skills. It was important that each student's superhero be focused on solving a problem and possess superpowers that related to the problem. As a class, students reviewed the following resources:

TED Talks: The Science of Superheroes

www.superheronation.com/2008/05/29/how-to-write-origin-
  stories/
www.newsarama.com/15572-the-10-best-superhero-origin-
  stories-of-all-time.html
www.readwritethink.org/resources/resource-print.
  html?id=30637

She then taught them how to fill in the fields on a Google Advanced Search page to obtain more information for their origin narratives.

Figure 5.7 shows an excerpt from Janet Han's origin narrative about Jimmy aka Galax.

Wolpert-Gawron had this to say about Janet:

> She's a bit of a success story in that she moved to this country only in 4th grade, was ELD through 6th, joined my Speech and Debate team in 7th and was also simultaneously moved to mainstream as an ELD3, and by 8th had gotten into ELA honors. We are convinced that by giving her access to some of the higher level classes and the speech team, she was able to listen, speak, and write at a very high quality from the get-go in middle school. Of course, she wouldn't have been able to do it had it not been for her work ethic and dedication to learning at the level of those students for whom she looked up to. As result, we all look up to her.

Once students had written their origin stories, the next step was to write an imaginary newspaper article describing their superhero in action. Wolpert-Gawron required a headline, a byline, an image, and the article, which had to include an interview quote

Figure 5.7. Excerpt from Origin Narrative

Jimmy opened the envelope and read the mysterious note:

"You are the one I have chosen to pass my superpower to. The superpower is to heal what have been hurt. And here is the bracelet that contains the power; there are few words you need to say before the superpower occurs. Heal what have been hurt, let your power shine. Your bracelet will shine while your superpower is on. Don't ever be a greedy person and brag about your superpower. If you did, your bracelet will turn red, and that's a signal for you to lose the power forever. Please remember that there is a limitation to the power, you can never ever harm anyone, or else the power will also be gone forever."

Then Jimmy left in the darkness. And as years went by Jimmy became Galax. He doesn't want Jimmy to be disappointed of him. So he used his power to heal the ones in need especially the ones who can't afford the money to see a doctor. Galax just felt meaningful after he saw the happy faces shown on people's face. He trained himself harshly and everyday he run his miles across the country just to have super speed so he can get to the patient's house as quickly as possible. He had dreamed and wanted to run faster and faster because every second matters. Maybe the god was impressed or maybe is just his luck, he unlock the secret to have enhanced speed.

Soon as he discovered those superpowers, his dream was to save the most people he could. And so he was well famous and everyone called Galax. A superhero. Galax knew the pain it was to lose somebody you loved for live. He knows how it feels and that's why he is here to help other not the feel the same way.

Source: Janet Han, 2014. Reprinted with permission.

from an eyewitness to the event. To ensure that students included the 5 Ws and H (Who, What, Where, When, Why, and How), she taught the "inverted pyramid" of newspaper writing. Many students created their visuals by hand, but others used the superhero creator on www.marvel.com.

It was now time to move to the argument genre. Wolpert-Gawron wanted her students to assume the persona of their superheroes and, in character, to address the United Nations. She approached the class this way:

> Continuing with our Superhero-themed semester, you will be presenting a series of issues to the United Nations. OK, so it won't be the real U.N., but we will be role-playing as our superheroes (yes, I fully expect costumes the day of your presentation) and as ambassadors for a particular country.

She then passed around a jar containing the names of each member nation and students selected them randomly. It was each student's job to research the nation he or she would be representing and to create a name plate with an appropriate symbol.

To focus students on their advocacy speeches, Wolpert-Gawron asked students to write a problem statement defining the broad problem or topic their superhero would address (e.g., world hunger, global warming, bullying, water pollution, etc.), listing three to five questions they had, and submitting a plan for how they would approach their speech, including sources of evidence. Students then wrote their advocacy speeches, which were required to include an introduction to the problem with a clear claim, research-based evidence with citations, how the problem related to the superhero, and a call to action. Figure 5.8 presents excerpts from each of the three sections of Janet Han's advocacy essay.

The essay was then condensed into 10 slides using Prezi, Google Presentation, or keynote. In costume, each student presented his or her argument (see Figure 5.9 for a photograph of one of Wolpert-Gawron's students in costume).

Figure 5.8. Superhero Advocacy Speech

Introduction

My fellow ambassadors, I wish to present a problem. A problem that sweeps the nation. A problem that spans the nation. A problem that a majority of Americans had experienced today. Over 53 million of people don't pay a visit to the doctor when they are needed because it's just too much for them to afford. One of the issues in the United States is poverty. The president, Barack Obama, and the government are currently working together and combating this current issue. As a matter of fact, somewhere in that coroner, poverty still remains. In the United States, others are showing no mercy to the poor and others treated them with unequally. Take this moment and think about all you know of poverty in the United States. Maybe you never recognize this problem because you never experience the things they experienced in your age. While you are enjoying your life, there are children out there who can't afford to go to school and receive an equal education, adults out there who can't find a job, and old grandpa and grandma still working out there in the fields. . . . I'm Galax and I lived in a poor village. A poor village that others treated us with biased visions. As the evidence I've collected, I believed that poverty is what we should all fight for.

Poverty is what we should fight for because we need to fight for equal chances and that we all deserve medical insurances. As a concluding point, remember no matter if you are poor or rich, we are all human beings. We must combat this issue and work together.

Evidence

Poverty in United States still remains, as a never ending story. I know how it feels to be one of the poor, and I feel passionate to talk to all of you about this issue in America. To furthermore explain my topic to fellows, let's look at some of the statistics:

One in six Americans lives in poverty due to the new census data dated November 6th, 2013. Without food stamps helping about 5 million people who were above the poverty line, the overall poverty rate would increase to 17.6 percent. Furthermore, the other statistics are collected according to Hunger in America. The evidenced revealed that my point of poverty in America still remains in America and continue to grow as one of the important factors in America. There are many researches, statistics, graphs that others conducted to show that the poverty remains in America and that the percentage of the poverty rate keep growing as the years went by. The next evidence is from *The New York Times*, "Poverty in America is Mainstream," written by Mark Rank. The following are some of the quotes in Mark Rank's article . . .

Call to action

I've proven to you all that poverty in the United States had been a huge event that spans the nation. Poverty led to no medical insurance, and to death. They are part of the poor and they don't receive equal visions. Others are biased, others are showing no mercy to the poverty. As I've stated, the poverty rate had been continuing growing. You can never predict your future. Now, we must fight and help the ones in need. Poverty needs us to help them. We must work together by writing our advocacy speech and perform around the world to others. Therefore, I would like to propose some solutions. First, we can start schools for the poor villages, and let the kids over there get educations. We can provide free transportation and secondly, we should start non-profit organizations which provides free foods, daily needs to the ones in need. And lastly, let's use technology to pass down our message. We need to let others be aware of this issue and concern about this problem currently sweeping the nation. Let's take our first step and begin now! Thank you, everyone.

Source: Janet Han, 2014. Reprinted with permission.

Figure 5.9. Superhero Advocacy Speech Presentation

Source: Heather Wolpert-Gawron, 2014. Reprinted with permission.

After watching live feed of proceedings from the real United Nations, students delivered their presentations before the classroom United Nations. The "ambassadors" in the audience listened from the lens of their specific country and posed questions both verbally and electronically, using mobile devices. Wolpert-Gawron read the back-channeling question threads and interjected, "The ambassador from _____ has a question for you." For example, Tiffany, representing Benin, asked: "How would you treat people in my country if we suffer from poverty and people can't afford treatment?" Speakers also took questions from the audience, saying, "I recognize the speaker from _____." In future iterations of this unit, Wolpert-Gawron plans to have ambassadors write "checks" to support the causes that were the most well-argued and for which the solutions were most convincing.

By enabling her students to adopt the persona of a superhero and invest themselves in researching an important problem for their superhero to investigate over an extended period of time and present before the "United Nations," Wolpert-Gawron created an engaging way to help students develop argumentative writing skills and to promote their cause in front of an audience of their peers. A day-to-day pacing guide and lesson plans for this ambitious unit will be featured in Wolpert-Gawron's newest book on project based learning, *DIY Project-Based Learning for ELA and History* (in press).

TRANSFORMING INFORMAL ENGLISH INTO ACADEMIC ENGLISH WITH OPINION ARGUMENT ON INFORMATIONAL TEXT

The CCSS require students to do more with academic language in text-based, argumentative writing than ever before (Zwiers et al., 2013). This type of writing plays a central role in their development of academic language across discipline areas (Council of Chief State Officers, 2012; Lee, Quinn, & Valdés, 2013; Schleppegrell, 2007). However, many ELs need daily instruction in academic language to support this development (Gersten et al., 2007). In the following activity students learn what academic language is expected in a formal argument on gun control. After reading two passages about gun control, one written by John Lott, Jr. (2003), and the other by Philip Cook and Kristin Goss (2014), students write an essay on their position on gun control. To teach students ways to use language to establish and maintain an academic style of writing, teachers can discuss the general characteristics of academic and informal writing and allow students to explore their differences. They can create two paragraphs, one written in informal English and the other written in academic English, seaming together portions of paragraphs that the students have already composed.

In analyzing student writing, we have found that the mistakes students make when writing formal essays involve deleting word endings, using slang and conversational vocabulary, and writing incomplete sentences. Figure 5.10 shows two sample paragraphs. One is written in informal English and the other in academic English. Students can work in pairs to complete a two-column chart (see Figure 5.11) in which they identify the informal and formal language features in both paragraphs. Giving students an answer key and asking them to discuss it after they have completed their charts increases their knowledge of academic language (Figure 5.12). Students can edit the informal paragraph on their own before editing their own writing, comparing their writing with the teacher's revised, more academic version, to make sure that they have used academic language consistently throughout their essays.

Figure 5.10. Two Sample Student Paragraphs for Students to Analyze

Directions: Read the following two student paragraphs carefully. Meet with a partner and discuss the two paragraphs. Write down specific examples from the essays to show why the first one is informal and the second one is more academic.

Student Paragraph 1 (Informal English)

John thinks that the goverment shuld give people the rights to own gun cuz of the law. But I don't agree. He's kinda wrong. And people like him sort of think that the goverment is stepping on rights. Goverment shuld not stop gun ownership. They think that most people who own guns are responsable guys who keep gun for sport and recreation, they also think that the police are unable to stop violent stuff, they think we need guns to protect ourselves. No way! I think he is wrong. So, I agree with Phil and Kristin. They think that guns increase bad crime. I also think that life is werth mor than having fun shooting targets with guns on the weekend. And I also think that many of the guns around the house are use by kids or teenagers killing themself. Anyway, guns are bad.

Student Paragraph 2 (Academic English)

Do individuals have the right to own guns? Drawing on the second Amendment of the Constitution, John Lott, Jr., political commentator and gun advocate, maintains in his book, *The Bias Against Guns,* that individuals have this right. This position asserts that the government infringes on our democratic rights when it restricts gun ownership. Most citizens who own guns, *so the argument goes,* keep guns for sports and recreation or self defense. *It is further contended that* the police are unable to stop violent crime and citizens need guns to protect themselves. However, as Philip Cook and Kristin Goss argue, in their book *The Gun Debate,* guns increase the number of violent crimes in the community. *Moreover,* many of the guns that are kept around the house end up being used in violent domestic disputes or teenage suicides. According to Cook and Goss, 30,000 Americans died from gun wounds in 2013. Few of these deaths related to self-defense or sports injuries. The evidence leads to the conclusion that gun control is necessary to reduce needless deaths related to crime, suicide, domestic disputes, and recreational accidents.

Students with moderate to advanced knowledge of English can compare entire papers written with informal and academic English.

Figure 5.11. Chart Comparing Informal Language with Academic Language

Write down specific examples from the essays to show why the first essay is informal and the second one is academic.

Informal	Academic

Figure 5.12. Sample Teacher Answer

Informal: Paragraph 1	Academic: Paragraph 2
Has spelling errors: (*goverment*) *government, (shuld) should, (responsable) responsible, (werth) worth, (mor) more, (themself) themselves*; *Cuz* should be *because*	Has no spelling errors
Has slang and colloquialisms: *guy, stuff, no way* *Anyway* and *by the way* are misplacement markers, which characterize oral language, not written	Doesn't have slang or colloquialisms
Uses an exclamation point: *No way!*	Does not use exclamation points.
Does not provide a hook to get the reader interested Doesn't introduce the readings	Begins with a question to hook the reader's attention
Mentions authors by first names (*John, Phil, Kristin*)	Introduces authors by their first and last name the first time they are mentioned, and then mentions them by their last names afterwards
Does not provide the reader with academic details about the readings	Provides the reader with the titles of the readings and their gist
Begins sentences with the word *and*; It should be deleted or replaced with a more academic word	Uses academic transition words like *moreover* instead of *and* to link ideas and sentences

Figure 5.12. Sample Teacher Answer (continued)

Informal: Paragraph 1	Academic: Paragraph 2
Begins sentences with the word *but*; which should be deleted or replaced with a more academic word	Uses academic transition words like *however* instead of *but*
Has hedges (*sort of* and *kind of*) that are common in everyday ordinary English	Does not use hedges
Has contractions (*don't; he's*)	Does not use contractions
Has grammaatical errors; deletes some word endings Has run-on sentences and comma splice errors like *They think that most people who own guns are responsable guys who keep gun for sport and recreation, they also think that the police are unable to stop violent stuff, they think we need guns to protect ourselves*	Does not have grammar errors
Overuse of words like *I think, I believe, In my opinion*; some teachers may feel that it is inappropriate in some, although not all, types of argumentative writing	Avoids using *I*. Uses impersonal language like *so the argument goes* and *maintains* to establish authority
Uses the same verbs like *state* repeatedly to discuss authors' views	Avoids needless repetition; uses a variety of academic reporting verbs like *maintains, argues, asserts,* and *contends* to discuss authors' views
Uses everyday, common words	Uses vivid and precise words and phrases: *political commentator, gun advocate, recreational injuries, domestic disputes*
Uses simple sentences	Uses academic grammar structures to sound informative and convey a proper tone, like *Drawing on*

Learning academic language through the activities above helps students improve both their academic reading and writing skills. Although ELs may be successful when communicating in informal contexts, they often struggle to communicate in writing in all their classrooms (Halliday, 2004), where the CCSS call for academic language to be used in writing. Learning the language forms valued in academic writing is a challenge for all students, but it is especially challenging for those with minimal exposure to such language and previous opportunities to learn it, such as ELs (Bailey, 2007; Schleppegrell, 2004). Research suggests that these learners will have difficulty comprehending their reading (Fillmore & Fillmore, 2012; Lesaux, Crosson, Kieffer, & Pierce, 2010) and developing proficiency in academic writing (Scarcella, 2003; Schleppegrell, 2007). Argumentative writing provides them with multiple opportunities to practice using academic language, and the activity above calls on them to develop their metalinguistic competence, the ability to think about academic language and analyze it for rhetorical effect. Such competence is critical in developing students' ability to edit their writing (Jessner, 2008).

To Sum Up

- Argumentative writing is at the core of most academic writing, yet most students, especially ELs, find it challenging.

- Argumentative writing presents both facts as well as reasoned opinions, and relies on supporting details to make its case.

- Arguments often take either an adversarial approach (Aristotelian) or a consensus-building approach (Rogerian). They can be broadly categorized as being either fact-based (using previous knowledge to derive claims, warrants, and evidence), judgment-based (defending and evaluating warrants explicitly), or policy-based (not only entailing explicit reference to the reasoning underlying warrants and claims but also suggesting a definite course of action).

- Common types of argumentative writing include expository writing, persuasive writing, analytical essays, rhetorical analysis, research papers, and personal essays.

- English learners, even those with intermediate to advanced levels of English language proficiency, will need instructional support to learn how to announce their topics and engage their readers, write strong thesis statements, link paragraphs and support with smooth transitions to make their writing cohesive, and use academic language.

References

Anstrom, K., DiCerbo, P., Butler, F., Katz, A., Millet, J., & Rivera, C. (2010). *A review of the literature on academic English: Implications for K–12 English language learners.* Arlington, VA: The George Washington University Center for Equity and Excellence in Education. Available at ceee.gwu.edu/Academic%20Lit%20Review_FINAL.pdf

Applebee, A. (2013). Common Core State Standards: The promise and the peril in a national palimpsest. *English Journal, 103,* 25–33.

Applebee, A. N., & Langer, J. A. (2011). A snapshot of writing instruction in middle schools and high schools. *English Journal, 100*(6), 14–27.

Applebee, A., Langer, J., Nystrand, M., & Gamoran, A. (2003). Discussion-based approaches to developing understanding: Classroom instruction and student performance in middle and high school English. *American Education Research Journal, 40*(3), 685–730.

Atwell, N. (1998). *In the middle: New understandings about writing, reading, and learning.* Portsmouth, NH: Boynton/Cook.

August, D. E., & Shanahan, T. E. (2006). *Developing literacy in second-language learners: Report of the National Literacy Panel on Language-Minority Children and Youth.* Mahwah, NJ: Erlbaum.

Bach, M. (2010). *The love letters of Henry VIII to Anne Boleyn.* Available at www.gutenberg.org/files/32155/32155-h/32155-h.htm

Baddeley A. (2003). Working memory: Looking back and looking forward. *Nature Reviews Neuroscience, 4,* 829–839.

Baddeley, A. D., & Hitch, G. J. (1974). Working memory. In G. A. Bower (Ed.), *The psychology of learning and motivation* (pp. 47–89). Waltham, MA: Academic Press.

Baddeley, A. D., & Hitch, G. J. (1994). Developments in the concept of working memory. *Neuropsychology, 8,* 485–493.

Bailey, A. L. (Ed.). (2007). *The language demands of school: Putting academic English to the test.* New Haven, CT: Yale University Press.

Baker, S., Lesaux, N., Jayanthi, M., Dimino, J., Proctor, C. P., Morris, J., . . . Newman-Gonchar, R. (2014). *Teaching academic content and literacy to English learners in elementary and middle school* (NCEE 2014-4012). Washington, DC: National Center for Education Evaluation and Regional Assistance (NCEE), Institute of Education Sciences, U.S. Department of Education. Available at ies.ed.gov/ncee/wwc/pdf/ practice_guides/english_learners_pg_040114.pdf

Ballantyne, K. G., Sanderman, A. R., & Levy, J. (2008). Educating English language learners: Building teacher capacity. Roundtable Report. *National Clearinghouse for English Language Acquisition & Language Instruction Educational Programs.*

Batalova, J., Fix, M., & Murray, J. (2007). *Measures of change: The demography and literacy of adolescent English learners—A report to the Carnegie Corporation of New York.* Washington, DC: Migration Policy Institute.

Batalova, J., & McHugh, M. (2010). *Top languages spoken by English language learners nationally and by state.* Washington, DC: Migration Policy Institute.

Bereiter, C., & Scardamalia, M. (1987). *The psychology of written composition.* Hillsdale, NJ: Erlbaum.

Biancarosa, C., & Snow, C. (2004). *Reading next—A vision for action and research in middle and high school literacy: A report to Carnegie Corporation of New York* (2nd ed.). Washington, DC: Alliance for Excellent Education.

Block, C. C., & Pressley, M. (Eds.). (2002). *Comprehension instruction: Research-based practices.* New York, NY: Guilford Press.

Bourdin, B., & Fayol, M. (1994). Is written language production more difficult than oral language production? A working memory approach. *International Journal of Psychology, 29,* 591–620.

Bradbury, R. (1998). All summer in a day. In *A medicine for melancholy and other stories.* New York, NY: HarperCollins.

Bruner, J. (1983). *Child's talk: Learning to use language.* New York, NY: W. W. Norton & Company.

Bruner, J. S. (2003). *Making stories: Law, literature, life.* Cambridge, MA: Harvard University Press.

Bunch, G. C. (2006). "Academic English" in the 7th grade: Broadening the lens, expanding access. *Journal of English for Academic Purposes, 5*(4), 284–301.

Bunch, G. C., Kibler, A., & Pimentel, S. (2012, January). *Realizing opportunities for English learners in the Common Core English Language Arts and Disciplinary Literacy Standards.* Paper presented at the Understanding Language Conference at Stanford University, Stanford, CA.

Capps, R., Fix, M., Murray, J., Ost, J., Passel, J. S., & Herawantoro, S. (2005). *The new demographics of American schools.* Washington, DC: The Urban Institute.

Chambliss, M. J., & Murphy, P. K. (2002). Fourth and fifth graders representing the argument structure in written texts. *Discourse Processes, 34*(1), 91–115.

Christie, F., & Macken-Horarik, M. (2007). Building verticality in subject English. In F. Christie & J. R. Martin (Eds.), *Language, knowledge, and pedagogy: Functional, linguistic, and sociological perspectives* (pp. 156–183). London, UK: Continuum.

Cisneros, S. (2002). Eleven. In *Woman Hollering Creek and other stories* (pp. 200–203). New York, NY: Vintage.

Cisneros, S. (2013). *The house on Mango Street.* New York, NY: Random House.

Coady, M., Hamann, E., Harrington, M., Pacheco, M., Pho, S., & Yedlin, J. (2003). *Claiming opportunities: A handbook for improving education for English language learners through comprehensive school reform.* Providence, RI: The Education Alliance at Brown University.

Coats, E. (n.d.). *Pixar's 22 rules to phenomenal storytelling* [PowerPoint presentation]. Available at www.slideshare.net/powerfulpoint/pixar-22rulestophenomenalstorytellingpowerfulpointslideshare

Collins, S. (2008). *The hunger games.* New York, NY: Scholastic Press.

Conley, M. W. (2008). Cognitive strategy instruction for adolescents: What we know about the promise, what we don't know about the potential. *Harvard Educational Review, 78*(1), 84–106.

Connor, U. (2008). Mapping multidimensional aspects of research. In U. Connor, E. Nagelhout, & W. V. Rozycki (Eds.), *Contrastive rhetoric: Reaching to intercultural rhetoric* (pp. 299–316). Philadelphia, PA: John Benjamins.

Connor, U. (2011). *Intercultural rhetoric in the writing classroom.* Ann Arbor: University of Michigan Press.

Cook, P. J., & Goss, K. A. (2014). *The gun debate: What everyone needs to know.* New York, NY: Oxford University Press.

Council of Chief State School Officers. (2012). *Framework for English language proficiency development standards corresponding to the Common Core State Standards and the next generation science standards.* Washington, DC: Author. Available at www.ccsso.org/Documents/2012/ELPD%20Framework%20Booklet-Final%20for%20web.pdf

Cumming, A. (2001). Learning to write in a second language: Two decades of research. *International Journal of English Studies, 1*(2), 1–23.

Cummins, J., & Yee-Fun, E. M. (2007). Academic language. In J. Cummins & C. Davison (Eds.), *International handbook of English language teaching* (pp. 797–810). New York, NY: Springer.

Cutler, L., & Graham, S. (2008). Primary grade writing instruction: A national survey. *Journal of Educational Psychology, 100*(4), 907–919.

D'Aoust, C. (1997). The saturation research paper. In C. B. Olson (Ed.), *Practical ideas for teaching writing as a process at the high school and college levels* (pp. 142–144). Sacramento, CA: California Department of Education.

Diaz, S., Moll, L. C., & Mehan, H. (1986). Sociocultural resources in instruction: A context-specific approach. In Bilingual Education Office, California State Department of Education (Ed.), *Beyond language: Social and cultural factors in schooling language minority students* (pp. 187–230). Los Angeles, California State University.

Donovan, M. (n.d.). 12 character writing tips for fiction writers. Available at www.writingforward.com/writing-tips/12-character-writing-tips-for-fiction-writers

Duke, N. K. (2004). The case for informational text. *Educational Leadership, 61*(6), 40–45.

Duke, N. K., Bennett-Armistead, V. S., & Roberts, E. M. (2002). Incorporating informational text in the primary grades. In C. Roller (Ed.), *Comprehensive reading instruction across the grade levels* (pp. 40–54). Newark, DE: International Reading Association.

Duke, N. K., Bennett-Armistead, V. S., & Roberts, E. M. (2003). Bridging the gap between learning to read and reading to learn. In D. M. Barone & L. M. Morrow (Eds.), *Literacy and young children: Research-based practices* (pp. 226–242). New York, NY: Guilford Press.

Duke, N. K., & Pearson, P. D. (2002). Effective practices for developing reading comprehension. In A. E. Farstrup & S. J. Samuels (Eds.), *What research has to say about reading instruction* (3rd ed., pp. 205–242). Newark, DE: International Reading Association.

Duke, N. K., & Purcell-Gates, V. (2003). Genres at home and at school: Bridging the known to the new. *The Reading Teacher, 57*(1), 30–37.

Echevarría, J., Vogt, M. E., & Short, D. J. (2012). *Making content comprehensible for English language learners: The SIOP model* (4th ed.). Boston, MA: Allyn & Bacon.

Ellis, R. (2009). Task-based language teaching: Sorting out the misunderstandings. *International Journal of Applied Linguistics, 19*(3), 221–246.

Ferretti, R. P., & Lewis, W. E. (2013). Best practices in teaching argumentative writing. In S. Graham, C. A. MacArthur, & J. Fitzgerald (Eds.), *Best practices in writing instruction* (2nd Ed., pp. 113–140). New York, NY: Guilford Press.

Ferris, D. (2011). *Treatment of error in second language student writing.* Ann Arbor: University of Michigan Press.

Ferris, D., & Hedgecock, J. (2013). *Teaching L2 composition: Purpose, process, and practice.* New York, NY: Routledge.

Fillmore, L. W., & Fillmore, C. J. (2012, January). What does text complexity mean for English learners and language minority students? Paper presented at the Understanding Language Conference, Stanford University. In K. Hakuta & M. Santos (Chairs), *Understanding language, literacy and learning in the content areas* (pp. 64–74). Stanford University. http://mes.sccoe.org/resources/ALI%202012/11_KenjiUL%20Stanford%20Final%205-9-12%20w%20cover.pdf

Fisher, D., & Frey, N. (2011). *Improving adolescent literacy: Content area strategies at work* (3rd ed.). Boston, MA: Allyn & Bacon.

Fitzgerald, J., & Amendum, S. (2007). What is sound writing instruction for multilingual learners? In S. Graham, C. A. MacArthur, & J. Fitzgerald (Eds.). *Best practices in writing instruction* (1st Edition, pp. 289–307). New York, NY: Guilford Press.

Fitzgerald, J., Olson, C. B., Garcia, S. G., & Scarcella, R. C. (2014). Assessing bilingual students' writing. In A. B. Clinton (Ed.), *Assessing bilingual children in context: An integrated approach* (pp. 215–240). Washington, DC: American Psychological Association.

Fitzgerald, J., & Shanahan, T. (2000). Reading and writing relations and their development. *Educational Psychologist, 35*(1), 39–50.

Flower, L. (1979). Writer-based prose: A cognitive basis for problems in writing. *College English, 41*(1), 19–37.

Flower, L. (1981). Revising writer-based prose. *Journal of Basic Writing, 3,* 62–74.

Flower, L., & Hayes, J. R., (1980). The dynamics of composing: Making plans and juggling constraints. In L. Gregg & E. Steinberg (Eds.), *Cognitive processes in writing* (pp. 31–50). Mahwah, NJ: Erlbaum.

Francis, D. J., Rivera, M., Lesaux, N., Keiffer, M., & Rivera, H. (2006). *Practical guidelines for the education of English language learners: Research-based recommendations for instruction and academic interventions.* Portsmouth, NH: Center on Instruction. Available at www.centeroninstruction.org/files/ELL1-Interventions.pdf

Frederiksen, C. H., & Dominic, J. F. (1981). Introduction: Perspectives on the activity of writing. In C. H. Frederiksen, & J. F. Dominic (Eds.), *Writing: The nature, development and teaching of written communication* (Vol. 2, pp. 1–20). Hillsdale, NJ: Erlbaum.

Fredricksen, J. E., Wilhelm, J. D., & Smith, M. W. (2012). *So, what's the story? Teaching narrative to understand ourselves, others, and the world.* Portsmouth, NH: Heinemann.

Fulkerson, R. (1996). *Teaching the argument in writing.* Urbana, IL: National Council of Teachers of English.

Gallagher, K. (2006). *Teaching adolescent writers.* Portland, ME: Stenhouse.

Gallagher, K. (2011). *Write like this: Teaching real-world writing through modeling and mentor texts.* Portland, ME: Stenhouse.

Gambrell, L. B. (1996). What research reveals about discussion. In L. B. Gambrell & J. F. Almasi (Eds.), *Lively discussions! Fostering engaged reading* (pp. 25–38). Newark, DE: International Reading Association.

Gambrell, L. B., Malloy, J. A., & Mazzoni, S. A. (2007). Evidence-based best practices for comprehensive literacy instruction. In L. B. Gambrell, L. M. Morrow, & M. Pressley (Eds.), *Best practices in literacy instruction* (3rd ed., pp. 1–29). New York, NY: Guilford Press.

Gándara, P. (1997*). Review of research on the instruction of limited English proficient students: A report to the California legislature.* Santa Barbara: University of California, Linguistic Minority Research Institute. Available at escholarship.org/uc/item/1133v9cc

Gándara, P., Rumberger, R., Maxwell-Jolly, J., & Callahan, R. (2003). ELs in California schools: Unequal resources, unequal outcomes. *Educational Policy Analysis Archives, 11*(36). Available at http://www.researchgate.net/publication/49610163_English_Learners_in_California_Schools_Unequal_resources_%27Unequal_outcomes

Gee, J. P. (2011). *Social linguistics and literacies: Ideology in discourses* (4th ed.). London, UK: Taylor & Francis.

Gersten, R., Baker, S. K., Shanahan, T., Linan-Thompson, S., & Collins, P. (2007). *Effective literacy and English language instruction for English learners in the elementary grades.* Washington, DC: Institute of Education Sciences, U.S. Department of Education.

Gibbons, P. (2002). *Scaffolding language, scaffolding learning: Teaching second language learners in the mainstream classroom.* Portsmouth, NH: Heinemann.

Gilbert, J., & Graham, S. (2010). Teaching writing to elementary students in grades 4–6: A national survey. *The Elementary School Journal, 110*(4), 494–518.

Goldenberg, C. (2008). Teaching English language learners: What the research does—and does not—say. *American Educator, 32,* 7–23, 42–44.

Goldenberg, C. (2012). Research on English learner instruction. In M. Calderon (Ed.), *Breaking through: Effective instruction and assessment for reaching English learners* (pp. 39–61). Bloomington, IN: Solution Tree Press.

Goldenberg, C. (2013). Unlocking the research on English learners: What we know—and don't yet know—about effective instruction. *American Educator, 37*(2), 4.

González, N., Moll, L., & Amanti, C. (2005). *Funds of knowledge: Theorizing practices in households, communities, and classrooms.* Mahwah, NJ: Lawrence Erlbaum Associates.

Graham, S. (2006). Strategy instruction and the teaching of writing: A meta-analysis. In C. A. MacArthur, S. Graham, & J. Fitzgerald (Eds.), *Handbook of writing research* (pp. 187–207). New York, NY: Guilford Press.

Graham, S., Bollinger, A., Booth Olson, C., D'Aoust, C., MacArthur, C., McCutchen, D., & Olinghouse, N. (2012). *Teaching elementary school students to be effective writers: A practice guide* (NCEE 2012-4058). Washington, DC: National Center for Education Evaluation and Regional Assistance (NCEE), Institute of Education Sciences, U.S. Department of Education. Available at ies.ed.gov/ncee/wwc/pdf/practice_guides/writing_pg_062612.pdf

Graham, S., Harris, K., & Hebert, M. (2011). Informing writing: The benefits of formative assessment. A report from Carnegie Corporation of New York. New York, NY: Carnegie Corporation of New York.

Graham, S., & Hebert, M. (2010). *Writing to read: Evidence for how writing can improve reading. A Carnegie Corporation time to act report.* Washington, DC: Alliance for Excellent Education.

Graham, S., & Perin, D. (2007). Writing next: Effective strategies to improve writing of adolescents in middle and high schools. A report to Carnegie Corporation of New York. *Alliance for Excellent Education.*

Greenleaf, C., Schoenbach, R., Cziko, C., & Mueller, F. (2001). Apprenticing adolescent readers to academic literacy. *Harvard Educational Review, 71*(1), 79–129.

Guthrie, J. T., & Wigfield, A. (2000). Engagement and motivation in reading. In M. Kamil & P. Mosenthal (Eds.), *Handbook of reading research* (Vol. 3, pp. 403–422). Mahwah, NJ: Erlbaum.

Gutiérrez, K. D. (1992). A comparison of instructional contexts in writing process classrooms with Latino children. *Education and Urban Society, 24*(2), 244–262.

Gutiérrez, K. D., Morales, P. Z., & Martinez, D. C. (2009). Re-mediating literacy: Culture, difference, and learning for students from non-dominant communities. *Review of Research in Education, 33*(1), 212–245.

Gutiérrez, K., & Vossoughi, S. (2010). Lifting off the ground to return anew: Documenting and designing for equity and transformation through social design experiments. *Journal of Teacher Education, 61*(1–2), 100–117.

Halliday, M. A. K. (Ed.). (2004). *Lexicology and corpus linguistics.* New York, NY: Bloomsbury Publishing.

Harklau, L., Losey, K. M., & Siegal, M. (Eds.). (1999). *Generation 1.5 meets college composition: Issues in the teaching of writing to U.S.-educated learners of ESL.* Mahwah, NJ: Lawrence Erlbaum Associates.

Harper, C., & Jong, E. (2004). Misconceptions about teaching English-language learners. *Journal of Adolescent & Adult Literacy, 48*(2), 152–162.

Hayes, J. R., & Flower, L. S. (1983). *A cognitive model of the writing process in adults. Final report*. National Institution of Education. Available at eric.ed.gov/?q=A+cognitive+model+of+the+writing+process+in+adults.+Final+report&id=ED240608

Heath, S. B. (1986). Taking a cross-cultural look at narratives. *Topics in Language Disorders, 7*(1), 84.

Hernandez, D. J., Denton, N. A., & Macartney, S. E. (2008). Children in immigrant families: Looking to America's future. *Social Policy Report, 22*(3), 3–22.

Hill, K. (Ed.). (2003). *Proceedings of the 2002 JALT Conference: Using discourse patterns to improve reading comprehension*. Tokyo, Japan: JALT Publications.

Hillocks, G. (2007). *Narrative writing: Learning a new model for teaching*. Portsmouth, NH: Heinemann.

Hillocks, G. (2011). *Teaching argument writing, grades 6–12: Supporting claims with relevant evidence and clear reasoning*. Portsmouth, NH: Heinemann.

Hornberger, N. H. (1989). Continua of biliteracy. *Review of Educational research, 59*(3), 271–296.

Horwitz, A., Uro, G., Price-Baugh, R., Simon, C., Uzzell, R., Lewis, S., & Casserly, M. (2009). *Succeeding with English language learners: Lessons learned from the Great City schools*. Available at http://files.eric.ed.gov/fulltext/ED508234.pdf

Hosseini, K. (2003). *The kite runner*. New York, NY: Penguin.

Hughes, L. (1993). Thank you, ma'am. In J. Trelease (Ed.), *Read all about it: Great read-aloud stories, poems, and newspaper* (pp. 82–92). New York, NY: Penguin Books.

Jessner, U. (2008). A DST model of multilingualism and the role of metalinguistic awareness. *The Modern Language Journal, 92*(2), 270–283.

Juel, C. (1994). *Learning to read and write in one elementary school*. New York, NY: Springer-Verlag.

Kellogg, R. T. (2008). Training writing skills: A cognitive developmental perspective. *Journal of Writing Research, 1*, 1–26.

Kim, J., Olson, C. B., Scarcella, R., Kramer, J., Pearson, M., van Dyk, D., . . . Land, R. (2011). Can a cognitive strategies approach to reading and writing instruction improve literacy outcomes for low income English language learners in the middle and high school grades? Results from a multi-site cluster, randomized controlled trial of the Pathway Project. *Journal of Research on Educational Effectiveness, 4,* 231–263.

Kirkpatrick, R., & Zang, Y. (2011). Correction: The negative influences of exam-oriented education on Chinese high school students: Backwash from classroom to child. *Language Testing in Asia, 4*(1), 2.

Kiuhara, S. A., Graham, S., & Hawken, L. S. (2009). Teaching writing to high school students: A national survey. *Journal of Educational Psychology, 101*(1), 136–160.

Kohn, A. (1996). *Beyond discipline: From compliance to community.* Alexandria, VA: Association for Supervision and Curriculum Development.

Kong, A., & Pearson, P. D. (2003). The road to participation: The construction of a literacy practice in a learning community of linguistically diverse learners. *Research in the Teaching of English, 38,* 85–124.

Krashen, S. D. (1993). *The power of reading: Insights from the research.* Englewood, CO: Libraries Unlimited.

Krathwohl, D. R., Bloom, B. S., & Masia, B. B. (1964). *Taxonomy of educational objectives: Book 2. Affective domain.* New York, NY: Longman.

Kuhn, D. (2005). *Education for thinking.* Cambridge, MA: Harvard University Press.

Labov, W. (1972). *Language in the inner city: Studies in the Black English vernacular* (Vol. 3). Philadelphia: University of Pennsylvania Press.

Labov, W., & Waletzky, J. (1967). Narrative analysis: Oral versions of personal experience. In J. Helm (Ed.), *Essays on the verbal and visual arts* (pp.12–44). Seattle: Washington University Press.

Langer, J. A. (1986). *Children reading and writing: Structures and strategies.* Norwood, NJ: Ablex.

Langer, J. A. (2002). *Effective literacy instruction: Building successful reading and writing programs.* Urbana, IL: National Council of Teachers of English.

Larmer, J., & Mergendoller, J. R. (2012). 8 essentials for project-based learning. *Buck Institute for Education.* Available at http://bie.org/object/document/8_essentials_for_project_based_learning

Larsen-Freeman, D. (1991). Second language acquisition research: Staking out the territory. *TESOL Quarterly, 25*(2), 315–350.

Lee, O., Quinn, H., & Valdés, G. (2013). Science and language for English language learners in relation to Next Generation Science Standards and with implications for Common Core State Standards for English language arts and mathematics. *Educational Researcher, 42*(4), 223–233.

Lesaux, N. K., Crosson, A. C., Kieffer, M. J., & Pierce, M. (2010). Uneven profiles: Language minority learners' word reading, vocabulary, and reading comprehension skills. *Journal of Applied Developmental Psychology, 31*(6), 475–483.

Lorenz, G. (1999). Learning to cohere: Causal links in native vs. non-native argumentative writing. In W. Bublitz, U. Lenk, & E. Ventola (Eds.), *Coherence in spoken and written discourse: How to create it and how to describe it.* Selected papers from the International Workshop on Coherence, Augsburg, 24–27 April 1997. Pragmatics and Beyond New Series, 55–76.

Lott Jr, J. R. (2003). *The bias against guns: Why almost everything you've heard about gun control is wrong.* Washington, DC: Regnery Publishing.

Magnier, M. (2011, March 17). For one quake survivor, self-help in the face of seeming helplessness. *Los Angeles Times.* Available at articles. latimes.com/2011/mar/17/world/la-fg-japan-quake-scuba-20110317

Margolis, R. (2007). Stranger in a strange land. *School Library Journal, 53*(9). Available at http://connection.ebscohost.com/c/ interviews/26519192/stranger-strange-land

Matsuda, P. K., Ortmeier-Hooper, C., & You, X. (Eds.). (2006). *The politics of second language writing: In search of the promised land.* West Lafayette, IN: Parlor Press.

Matsuda, P. K., & Silva, T. (Eds.). (2005). *Second language writing research: Perspectives on the process of knowledge construction.* Mahwah, NJ: Erlbaum.

Matuchniak, T. (2013). *Mind the gap: A cognitive strategies approach to college writing readiness for English language learners.* Irvine: University of California, Irvine.

Matuchniak, T., Olson, C. B., & Scarcella, R. (2014). Examining the text-based, on-demand, analytical writing of mainstreamed Latino English learners in a randomized controlled field trial of the Pathway Project intervention. *Reading and Writing: An Interdisciplinary Journal, 27*(6), 973–994.

McCann, T. M. (1989). Student argumentative writing knowledge and ability at three grade levels. *Research in the Teaching of English, 23,* 62–76.

McCutchen, D. (1988). "Functional automaticity" in children's writing: A problem of metacognitive control. *Written Communication, 5,* 306–324.

Meltzer, J., & Hamann, E. T. (2005). *Meeting the literacy development needs of adolescent English language learners through content area learning. Part two: Focus on classroom teaching and learning strategies.* Providence, RI: The Education Alliance at Brown University. Available at www.brown.edu/academics/education-alliance/sites/brown.edu.aca-demics.education-alliance/files/publications/adell_litdv2.pdf

Menken, K., & Kleyn, T. (2009). The difficult road for long-term English learners. *Educational Leadership, 66*(7). Available at www.ascd. org/publications/educational_leadership/apr09/vol66/num07/The_ Difficult_Road_for_Long-Term_English_Learners.aspx

Meyer, B. J. (1985). Signaling the structure of text. *The Technology of Text, 2,* 64–89.

Meyer, B. J. (2003). Text coherence and readability. *Topics in Language Disorders, 23*(3), 204–224.

Ministry of Education of the People's Republic of China. (2011). English Curriculum Standards for Compulsory Education (2011 version). Beijing, China: Beijing Normal University Press.

National Commission on Writing for America's Families, Schools and Colleges. (2003). *The neglected "R": The need for a writing revolution.* Available at www.nwp.org/cs/public/print/resource/2523

National Governors Association Center for Best Practices & Council of Chief State School Officers. (2010). *Common Core State Standards for English Language Arts and Literacy in History/Social Studies, Science, and Technical Subjects.* Washington, DC: Authors. Available at http://www.corestandards.org/ELA-Literacy/

National Institute of Child Health and Human Development. (2000). *Report of the National Reading Panel. Teaching children to read: An evidence-based assessment of the scientific research literature on reading and its implications for reading instruction* (NIH Publication No. 00-4769). Washington, DC: U.S. Government Printing Office.

New London Group. (1996). A pedagogy of multi-literacies: Designing social futures. *Harvard Educational Review, 66*(1), 60–92.

Noden, H. R. (2011). *Image grammar: Teaching grammar as part of the writing process.* Portsmouth, NH: Heinemann.

Norris, J. M., & Ortega, L. (2000). Effectiveness of L2 instruction: A research synthesis and quantitative meta-analysis. *Language learning, 50*(3), 417–528.

Olsen, L. (2010). A closer look at long term English learners: A focus on new directions. *In the STARlight: Research and Resources for English Learner Achievement* (7). Available at en.elresearch.org/issues/7

Olson, C. B. (Ed.). (1992). *Thinking/writing: Fostering critical thinking through writing.* New York, NY: HarperCollins College Division.

Olson, C. B. (1997). Practical ideas for assigning the saturation report. In C. B. Olson (Ed.), *Practical ideas for teaching writing as a process at the high school and college levels* (pp. 138–144). Sacramento, CA: California Department of Education.

Olson, C. B. (2011). *The reading/writing connection: Strategies for teaching and learning in the secondary classroom* (3rd ed.). Boston, MA: Allyn & Bacon.

Olson, C. B., Kim, J. S., Scarcella, R., Kramer, J., Pearson, M., van Dyk, D., Collins, P., & Land, R. (2012). Enhancing the interpretive reading and analytical writing of mainstreamed English learners in secondary school: Results from a randomized field trial using a cognitive strategies approach. *American Educational Research Journal, 4*(2), 323–355.

Olson, C. B., & Land, R. (2007). A cognitive strategies approach to reading and writing instruction for English language learners in secondary school. *Research in the Teaching of English, 41*(3), 269–303.

Olson, C. B., Land, R., Anselmi, T., & AuBuchon, C. (2010). Teaching secondary English learners to understand, analyze, and write interpretive essays about theme. *Journal of Adolescent & Adult Literacy, 54*(4), 245–256.

Olson, C. B., Scarcella, R., & Matuchniak, T. (2013). Best practices in teaching writing to English learners: Reducing constraints to facilitate writing development. In S. Graham, C. A. MacArthur, & J. Fitzgerald (Eds.), *Best practices in writing instruction* (2nd ed., pp. 381–402). New York, NY: Guilford Press.

Ortega, L. (2003). Syntactic complexity measures and their relationship to L2 proficiency: A research synthesis of college-level L2 writing. *Applied Linguistics, 24,* 492–518.

Ortega, L. (2009). Sequences and processes in language learning. In M. H. Long & C. J. Doughty (Eds.), *The handbook of language teaching* (pp. 81–105). Oxford, UK: Wiley-Blackwell.

Panofsky, C., Pacheco, M., Smith, S., Santos, J., Fogelman, C., Harrington, M., & Kenney, E. (2005). *Approaches to writing instruction for adolescent English language learners: A discussion of recent research and practice literature in relation to nationwide standards on writing.* Providence, RI: The Education Alliance at Brown University.

Paris, S. G., Wasik, B., & Turner, J. C. (1991). The development of strategic readers. In R. Barr, M. L. Kamil, P. Mosenthal, & P. D. Pearson (Eds.), *Handbook of reading research* (Vol. 2, pp. 609–640). New York, NY: Longman.

Partnership for 21st Century Skills. (2008). 21st century skills English map. Available at www.p21.org/storage/documents/21st_century_skills_english_map.pdf

Pearson, P. D., & Gallagher, M. C. (1983). The instruction of reading comprehension. *Contemporary Educational Psychology, 8*(3), 317–344.

Pennycook, A. (2001). *Critical applied linguistics: A critical introduction.* Mahwah, NJ: Lawrence Erlbaum Associates.

Perie, M., Grigg, W., & Donahue, P. (2005). *The nation's report card: Reading 2005, 4.*

Persky, H., Daane, M., & Jin, Y. (2003). *The nation's report card: Writing 2002.* Washington, DC: National Center for Education Statistics, U.S. Department of Education.

Pike, K., & Mumper, J. (2004). *Making nonfiction and other informational texts come alive: A practical approach to reading, writing, and using nonfiction and other informational texts across the curriculum.* Boston, MA: Pearson Education.

Pitts, L. (2010, January 14). Sometimes, the earth is cruel. *The Dallas Morning News.* Available at www.dallasnews.com/opinion/latest-columns/20100114-Leonard-Pitts-Sometimes-the-9424.ece

Polio, C., & Williams, J. (2009). Teaching and testing writing. In M. Long & C. Doughty (Eds.), *The handbook of language teaching* (pp. 486–517). Oxford, UK: Blackwell.

Purcell-Gates, V., Duke, N. K., Hall, L. A., & Tower, C. (2002, December). *Text purposes and text use: A case for elementary science instruction.* In W. H. Teale (Chair), Relationships between text and instruction: Evidence from three studies. Paper presented at the annual meeting of the National Reading Conference, Miami, FL.

Raphael, T. E., Englert, C. S., & Kirschner, B. W. (1989). Students' metacognitive knowledge about writing. *Research in the Teaching of English, 23,* 343–379.

Rivera, M. O., Francis, D. J., Fernandez, M., Moughamian, A. C., Lesaux, N. K., & Jergensen, J. (2010). *Effective practices for English language learners. Principals from five states speak.* Portsmouth, NH: RMC Research Corporation, Center on Instruction. Available at centeroninstruction.org/files/Effective%20Practices%20for%20ELLs.pdf

Roberge, M., Siegal, M., & Harklau, L. (2009). *Generation 1.5 in college composition: Teaching academic writing to U.S.-educated learners of ESL.* New York, NY: Routledge.

Roberts, K. L., Norman, R. R., Duke, N. K., Morsink, P., Martin, N. M., & Knight, J. A. (2013). Diagrams, timelines, & tables, oh my! Concepts and comprehension of graphics. *The Reading Teacher, 61,* 12–24.

Rogoff, B. (1990). *Apprenticeship in thinking: Cognitive development in social context.* New York, NY: Oxford University Press.

Rosenblatt, R. (1982, January 25). The man in the water. *Time.* Available at content.time.com/time/magazine/article/0,9171,925257,00.html

Roth, V. (2011). *Divergent.* New York, NY: HarperCollins.

Rylant, C. (1982). *When I was young in the mountains.* New York, NY: Dutton.

Salahu-Din, D., Persky, H., & Miller, J. (2008). *The nation's report card: Writing 2007.* Washington, DC: National Center for Education Statistics.

Scarcella, R. (2003). *Academic English: A conceptual framework* (Tech. Rep. No. 2003-1). Irvine: University of California, Irvine, University of California Linguistic Minority Research Institute.

Schleppegrell, M. J. (2004). *The language of schooling: A functional linguistics perspective.* Mahwah, NJ: Erlbaum.

Schleppegrell, M. J. (2007). The linguistic challenges of mathematics teaching and learning: A research review. *Reading & Writing Quarterly, 23*(2), 139–159.

Schleppegrell, M. J. (2009, October). Language in academic subject areas and classroom instruction: What is academic language and how can we teach it? Paper presented at workshop on *The role of language in school learning* sponsored by the National Academy of Sciences, Menlo Park, CA. Available at https://www.mydigitalchalkboard.org/cognoti/content/file/resources/documents/98/98c3e7f4/98c3e7f49b44eaa5ee60b45939df619b4593afc7/Schleppegrell.pdf

Schleppegrell, M. J. (2013). The role of metalanguage in supporting academic language development. *Language Learning, 63*(1), 153–170.

Shanahan, T., & Shanahan, C. (2008). Teaching disciplinary literacy to adolescents: Rethinking content-area literacy. *Harvard Educational Review, 78*(1). Available at www.missionliteracy.com/uploads/3/1/5/8/3158234/teaching_disciplinary_literacy_shanahan_2008.pdf

Short, D., & Fitzsimmons, S. (2007). *Double the work—Challenges and solutions to acquiring language and academic literacy for adolescent English language learners: A report to Carnegie Corporation of New York.* Washington, DC: Alliance for Excellent Education.

Smith, M. W., & Wilhelm, J. D. (2002). *"Reading don't fix no Chevys": Literacy in the lives of young men.* Portsmouth, NH: Heinemann.

Smith, M. W., Wilhelm, J. D., & Fredricksen, J. E. (2012). *Oh yeah?! Putting argument to work both in school and out.* Portsmouth, NH: Heinemann.

Snow, C. E., & Beals, D. E. (2006). Mealtime talk that supports literacy development. *New Directions for Child and Adolescent Development, 2006*(111), 51–66.

Snow, C., & Biancarosa, G. (2003). *Adolescent literacy and the achievement gap: What do we know and where do we go from here?* New York, NY: Carnegie Corporation.

Snow, C. E., & Uccelli, P. (2009). The challenge of academic language. In N. Torrance & D. R. Olson (Eds.), *The Cambridge handbook of literacy* (pp. 112–133). New York, NY: Cambridge University Press.

Soto, G. (1990). Seventh grade. In G. Soto (Ed.), *Baseball in April* (pp. 52–59). Orlando, FL: Harcourt.

Street, B. V. (2005). *Literacies across educational contexts: Mediating learning and teaching.* Philadelphia, PA: Caslon Publishing.

Tan, S. (2007). *The arrival.* New York, NY: Arthur A. Levine Books.

Tchudi, S., & Mitchell, D. (1999). *Exploring and teaching the English language arts* (4th ed.). New York, NY: Longman.

Tharp, R. G., & Gallimore, R. (1991). *The instructional conversation: Teaching and learning in social activity.* Santa Cruz, CA: University of California, Center for Research on Education, Diversity & Excellence.

Tierney, R. J., & Pearson, P. D. (1983). Toward a composing model of reading. *Language Arts, 60*(5), 568–580.

Tierney, R. J., & Shanahan, T. (1991). Research on the reading–writing relationship: Interactions, transactions, and outcomes. In R. Barr, M. Kamil, P. Mosenthal, & P. D. Pearson (Eds.), *Handbook of reading research* (Vol. 2, pp. 246–280). New York, NY: Longman.

Tierney, R. J., Soter, A., O'Flahavan, J., & McGinley, W. (1989). The effects of reading and writing upon thinking critically. *Reading Research Quarterly, 24*(2), 134–173.

Tompkins, G. E. (2013). *Literacy for the twenty-first century: A balanced approach* (6th ed.). Upper Saddle River, NJ: Pearson.

Treat, L. (1982). *Crime and puzzlement 2: More solve-them-yourself picture mysteries.* Boston, MA: David R. Godine.

Uccelli, P., Hemphill, B. A., Pan, B. A., & Snow, C. E. (2005). Conversing with toddlers about the nonpresent. Precursors to narrative development in two genres. In C. S. Tamis-LeMonda (Ed.), *Child psychology. A handbook of contemporary issues* (pp. 215–237). Philadelphia, PA: Psychology Press.

U.S. Department of Education, Institute of Education Sciences, National Center for Education Statistics. (2012a). *Digest of education statistics 2012.* Table 47. Number and percentage of public school students participating in programs for English language learners, by state: Selected years, 2002–03 through 2010–11. Washington, DC: Author. Available at nces.ed.gov/programs/digest/d12/tables/dt12_047.asp

U.S. Department of Education, Institute of Education Sciences, National Center for Education Statistics. (2012b). *The nation's report card: Writing 2011* (NCES 2012-470). Washington, DC: Author.

Valdés, G. (2001). *Learning and not learning English: Latino students in American schools.* New York, NY: Teachers College Press.

Valdés, G., Kibler, A., & Walqui, A. (2014). *Changes in the expertise of ESL professionals: Knowledge and action in an era of new standards.* Alexandria, VA: TESOL International Association.

van Lier, L., & Walqui, A. (2012, January). How teachers and educators can most usefully and deliberately consider language. Paper presented at the Understanding Language Conference, Stanford, CA. Available at ell.stanford.edu/publication/language-and-common-core-state-standards

Villegas, A. M., & Lucas, T. (2002). Preparing culturally responsive teachers rethinking the curriculum. *Journal of Teacher Education, 53*(1), 20–32.

Vygotsky, L. S. (1986). *Thought and language*. Cambridge, MA: MIT Press. (Original work published in 1934)

Warschauer, M. (2009). Digital literacy studies: Progress and prospects. In M. Baynham & M. Prinsloo (Eds.), *The future of literacy studies* (pp. 123–140). New York, NY: Palgrave Macmillan.

Wilhelm, J. D. (2001). *Improving comprehension with think-aloud strategies*. New York, NY: Scholastic.

Wilhelm, J. D., Smith, M. W., & Fredricksen, J. E. (2012). *Get it done! Writing and analyzing informational texts to make things happen*. Portsmouth, NH: Heinemann.

Williams, C., Stathis, R., & Gotsch, P. (2009). *Managing student talk in the English language development classroom*. Ruidoso, NM: Teacher Writing Center. Available at www.teacherwritingcenter.org/ Managing_Student_Talk_V5.pdf

Wolpert-Gawron, H. (2014). *Writing behind every door: Teaching Common Core writing in the content areas*. New York, NY: Routledge.

Wolpert-Gawron, H. (in press). *DIY project-based learning for ELA and history*. New York, NY: Routledge.

Wong Fillmore, L., & Snow, C. (2003). What teachers need to know about language. In C. T. Adger, C. E. Snow, & D. Christian (Eds.), *What teachers need to know about language* (pp. 10–46). McHenry, IL: Center for Applied Linguistics.

Woodrell, D. (2007). *Winter's bone: A novel*. New York, NY: Hachette Digital.

Wulff, J. (September 18, 2006). Wild by nature. *People, 66*(12). Available at http://www.people.com/people/archive/article/0,,20060360,00.html

Yuan, F., & Ellis, R. (2003). The effects of pre-task planning and on-line planning on fluency, complexity and accuracy in L2 oral production. *Applied Linguistics, 24*, 1–27.

Ziergiebel, A. M. (2013). Digital literacy in practice: Achieving a cosmopolitan orientation. In J. Ippolito, J. F. Lawrence, & C. Zaller (Eds.), *Adolescent literacy in the era of the common core: From research into practice* (pp. 131–142). Cambridge, MA: Harvard Education Press.

Zwiers, J. (2008). *Building academic language: Essential practices for content classrooms*. San Francisco, CA: Jossey-Bass.

Zwiers, J., O'Hara, S., & Pritchard, R. (2013). *Eight essential shifts for teaching Common Core Standards to academic English learners*. Stanford, CA: Academic Language Development Network. Available at aldnetwork.org/news/eight-essential-shifts-teaching-common-core-standards-academic-english-learners

Index

The appearance of *f* or *t* after a page number denotes figure or table respectively.

About the Authors

Carol Booth Olson is an associate professor in the School of Education at the University of California, Irvine, and director of the UCI site of the National Writing Project. Olson is an expert in the field of reading and writing and has authored five books and over 30 articles on effective literacy instruction. She has been an expert panelist for a What Works Clearinghouse practice guide on writing instruction (Graham et al., 2012) and is the recipient of two state and two national awards for outstanding educational research to improve the academic literacy of English learners.

Robin C. Scarcella is a professor in the School of Humanities at the University of California, Irvine, and director of the Program in Academic English. Scarcella is a linguist who specializes in strategies for accelerating the academic English of ELs, also the title of her most recent book (2003). She has contributed to the creation of California's ELD Standards, served as an expert panelist for a What Works Clearinghouse practice guide on research-based practices for teaching ELs (Gersten et al., 2007), and written over 25 journal articles and four books.

Tina Matuchniak is the director of research for the UCI Writing Project at the University of California, Irvine, and a lecturer at California State University, Long Beach. Matuchniak specializes in language and literacy, specifically as they apply to the needs and practices of English learners. She has authored several articles and book chapters and has been recognized for excellence in teaching and research through multiple awards and fellowships.